A HISTORY *of* IDUMA

FROM ANCIENT TIMES

by

COLLINS EBI DANIEL

Published in 2017 by Onyoma Research Publications
11 Orogbum Crescent, GRA Phase II
P.O. Box 8611, Federal Secretariat Post Office, Port Harcourt, Rivers State, Nigeria.
E-mail: kala_joe@yahoo.com   Mobile Phone: +234 (0) 803-308-3385

Website: www.onyomaresearch.com

Copyright © **Collins E. Daniel, 2017**

Cover Design   **Samuel Marshall**

Proofreading, Formatting and Indexing   **Sotonye Afiesimama**

Website: www.sotonye.com/edit

ISBN 978-978-8195-66-5

All rights reserved. No part of this publication may be reproduced, stored in a retrieval system o r transmitted in any form or by any means, electronic, mechanical, photocopying, recording, or otherwise without the prior permission in writing from the author, except by a reviewer or writ er who may quote a brief passage. Application for other use of copyright material including permission to reproduce extracts in other published works shall be made to the publisher full acknowledgement of author, publisher and source must be given.

DEDICATION

I dedicate this book to my beloved parents
Mr. Ebimawoto Daniel
&
Mrs. Elizabeth Offor Daniel
of blessed memory
for their
care, guidance, love and support.

ACKNOWLEDGEMENTS

This work has been made possible by the Almighty God through whom I derived inspiration, grace and guidance in writing this book.

I am thankful to Emeritus Professor E. J. Alagoa of the University of Port Harcourt in many ways: firstly, for his willingness to be part of this project, and who read the initial draft and made some insightful and useful comments; secondly, he made me to dig deeper and deeper to find the jewels awaiting there; thirdly, for accepting to write the foreward to this book when I approached him, without any hesitation. I am indeed grateful to him for all of these, especially his love for scholarship and constant encouragement. I remain much indebted and do indeed appreciate.

My appreciation also goes to Emeritus Professor Robin Horton, formerly of the History Department, University of Port Harcourt, who supervised my earlier work on the subject, for his constant encouragement. That earlier work which could not be published formed the cornerstone for this book.

I wish to also appreciate two royal fathers in Iduma, HRH Felix E. Aboko-Igoniwari the XII, (JP), the Olilaema of Idema, and HRH Simeon M. Ake-Opuso, the Olilaema of Obeduma, for their various positive roles, support and encouragement in the course of writing this book.

I must not forget to mention my good friend Mr. Sokariye Dan-Sokari of Ke through whom I had access to chiefs and elders of Ke who volunteered historical information to me at different sessions in Ke town.

To Captain Glory E. Koru (rtd.), I very much appreciate the historical information and insights you have shared with me. I must thank you for your willingness to respond to so many questions I had intermittently put to you, some at odd times.

I must also thank Prince Sokari Adewari and Chief Isu Otolo-Oga of blessed memory, for their wide knowledge of I duma history and economy, including other matters of historical significance which they readily shared with me in the course of my research.

To my secretariat personnel, especially Margdalene Oti, Tonworio F. Amaegbe, I acknowledge your commitment and devotion in typing the manuscript. This work would have been further delayed without your effort.

Finally, I must not fail to specially acknowledge my family as this work would not have been possible without the understanding, support and encouragement of my wonderful and cherished family. In spite of the demands of the throne, the family remains a pillar of support and encouragement, which made me focused. I remain grateful to you all, and do very much cherish and appreciate your understanding.

Collins Ebi Daniel

ABBREVIATIONS

AG   - ACTION GROUP

AAAP   - AGGRESSIVE AGRARIAN AGRICULTURAL POLICY

CGS   - CHIEF OF GENERAL STAFF

COR   - CROSS RIVERS, OGOJA, RIVERS

GMOU - GENERAL MEMORANDUM OF UNDERSTANDING

MORETO - MOVEMENT FOR REPARATION TO OGBIA

NA - NATIVE AUTHORITY

NPN - NATIONAL PARTY OF NIGERIA

NCNC - NATIONAL COUNCIL OF NIGERIA AND THE CAMEROUNS

NPC - NORTHERN PEOPLES CONGRESS

NAOC - NIGERIAN AGIP OIL COMPANY

NDDC - NIGER DELTA DEVELOPMENT COMMISSION

NNA - NIGERIA NATIONAL ALLIANCE

NNDP - NIGERIA NATIONAL DEMOCRATIC PARTY

OFN - OPERATION FEED THE NATION

PRC - PROVISIONAL RULING COUNCIL

UMBC - UNITED MIDDLE BELT CONGRESS

UPGA - UNITED PROGRSSIVE GRAND ALLIANCE

RCPC - RIVERS CHIEFS AND PEOPLES CONFERENCE

RPL - RIVERS PEOPLES LEAGUE

RNC - ROYAL NIGER COMPANY

SPDC - SHELL PETROLEUM DEVELOPMENT COMPANY

FOREWORD

This book, *A History of Iduma from Ancient Times,* has come out of the very deepest experiences of the life of the author . He clearly rose out of the local rural environment, in the midst of the traditions and culture of the community. By t he time he came to the University of Port Harcourt as a his tory student, he was already a part of my own view of hist ory as an integral part of the life and culture of the people about whom the historian tells the story.

The book, *A History of Iduma from Ancient Times,* has alread y gone beyond the years of the author as a history student and graduate of history. He has gone out into the world to earn other degrees, acquired additional competences, and achieved greater laurels, all of which should have improved his awareness for diversity of sources and view points, and variant versions of traditions. His legal practice after a history degree and practical experience must be counted additional assets, crowned with his acceptance of a traditional leadership position over the Abureni Clan.

It has been my good fortune to teach students who have come out with a passion to make their own contributions in the field. I recommend this book to the reading public and urge all readers to be rigorous and critical in their reading and assessment of the product. The historian uses diverse sources and records, but the final story and interpretations of the documents belong to the historian. He must accept full, final responsibility.

I congratulate King Collins Ebi Daniel, the paramount ruler of Abureni Clan, for his brave effort to tell the story of his home community of Iduma. I recommend it to readers throughout the Niger Delta, Nigeria and the global community. A good historical account has something relevant to teach all readers.

Emeritus Professor Ebiegberi Joe Alagoa,
NNOM, OON, FNAL, FHSN

TABLE of CONTENTS

Dedication iii
Acknowledgement iv
Abbreviations vii
Foreword ix
Table of Contents xii

Chapter 1
General Introduction 1
1.1 Aim of Study and Method 1
1.2 Location, Environment and People 3
1.3 Community Organisation and Architecture 8
1.4 Literature Review 11
1.5 Sources and Problems 17

Chapter 2
Origin, Migrations and Settlement 21
2.1(i) The Idema (Aye)/Eboh Version 21
2.1(ii) The Opuso Version 29
2.1(iii) The Awo Version 31
2.2 A Critical Appraisal of the Traditions 33
2.3 Chronology 41

Chapter 3

Economic organization in pre-colonial era
(1400AD – 1800AD) 44
1.1 Land Tenure and Farming 44
1.2 Palm Oil and Kernel Production 48
1.3 Raffia Products 53
1.4 Canoe/paddle Production 55
1.5 Hunting 57
1.6 Fishing 59
1.7 Trading 61

Chapter 4
Socio-political Organizations in the Pre-colonial Era
(1400AD – 1800AD) 63
4.1 The Family (Eghun) 63
4.2 The House (Oghol-Otu) 66
4.3 The Village (Ema) 67
4.4 Town/Village-wide Institutions 72
4.5 Economy and Society 74

Chapter 5
Iduma in the period before colonial rule
(1800 – 1899) 19th century 78
5.1 Economic Changes 78
5.2 The Impact of the 1895 Akassa War 95
5.3 Political Developments 102
5.4 Economy and Society 105

Chapter 6
Iduma from the beginning of colonial rule to independence
(1900 – 1960) 108
6.1 Political Developments 109
6.2 Economic Changes 124
6.3 Social Changes 129
6.4 Economy and Society 134

Chapter 7

Iduma after Nigeria independence (1960 – 1996)   **137**
7.1   Political Developments in Nigeria   138
7.2   Political Developments in Iduma   164
7.3   Social and Economic Changes   185
7.4   Impact of Nigerian Civil War   197

Chapter 8
Iduma since the creation of Bayelsa State (1996 – 2017)   **207**
8.1   Political Developments   209
8.2   Social and Economic changes   222
8.3   Iduma in Ogbia Brotherhood   237

Chapter 9
External Relations with Neighbours   **240**
9.1   Iduma and her Abureni Neighbours   240
9.2   External Relations with other Neighbours   247

Chapter 10
Summary and Conclusion   **260**

Appendices
Appendix I   Family Tree of the Central Delta Group   266
Appendix II   King List and Genealogy   267
Appendix III   King List and Genealogy of Idema   269
Appendix IV   King List/ Traditional Leaders of Eboh   271

Appendix V   King List/ Traditional Rulers of Obeduma   273
Appendix VI   Primary Sources   275

Glossary   **280**

Bibliography   **283**

Index   **288**

CHAPTER 1
GENERAL INTRODUCTION

1.1 Aim of study and methods

This work is an attempt to reconstruct the history of Iduma from their own tradition. Though, earlier work done on Iduma could not be published for reasons unconnected with the desire for more detailed research. That notwithstanding, the documentation of the history of Iduma is rather overdue and has become more compelling in view of its special features: (i) Iduma as a melting point of three cultures – Kalabari-Ijo, Ogbia and Odual, (ii) Its strategic location, as a buffer zone between two hitherto powerful coastal city states of Kalabari (New Calabar) and Brass. (iii) As a community that shares both the fresh and salt water geographical vegetation.

The city states of Kalabari and Brass played significant roles and indeed dominated both the slave trade and the palm oil and kernel trade. Iduma was a major producer community in the case of the latter trade. The contributio ns of Iduma therefore, deserve a proper study and documentation.

Apart from examining the general history of the people, one cardinal objective would be to show the changing patterns of economic activities in relation to the new demands, resulting from the influence of three external powers: Kalabari (New Calabar), Nembe and the British. It will examine the influence of the economy on social political organization.

The work will further examine the self determination of the Iduma people to break loose from Nembe political hegemony to join her kith and kin in the Ogbia Local Government Council under an autonomous Abureni Clan.

It will also examine the political, social and economic developments of Iduma since the creation of Bayelsa State, including its special place in Ogbia Brotherhood. And finally, it will examine Iduma relations with her neighbours over the period.

In a study of this nature, since there are few written records covering the periods before the 19th century, studi es of these periods have as a result of necessity, almost solely relied on oral tradition, as a source material.

In doing all of these, I have carefully adopted a periodisation of the events that suits the presentation to achieve the aim of the study.

1.2 Location, Environment and People

Iduma is situated in Ogbia Local Government Area in Bayelsa State, Nigeria. Its geographical co-ordinates are 4° 37' 55"North, and 6°27'35" East[1].

Iduma is bounded on the North by Kugbo and Odual, North West by Otuabagi-Ogbia, South by Odioma and Kula, South West by Nembe, West by Okoroba and East by the Kalabaris (Abonnema, Soku and Sangama).

The people occupy a low lying land of less than 20 meters above sea level. In the rainy season, the water level

---

1. See "http:www.maplandia.com/Nigeria/rivers/brass/idema/"title="google satellite map. Accessed 7th November 2016

rises as high as 4ft above the water level and receeds to its barest minimum during the dry season.

They are settled in seven main communities namely: Idema, Iduma, Eboh, Obeduma, Emalo, Oruan (Atubo I), and Oboghe (Adigiasikolo) aside from several other satellite settlements hidden within the numerous creeks of the Niger Delta. The Idema creek is one of these small creeks leading out of the Brass estuary. The maze of intercommunicating channels which dissect the area open to the Atlantic by several mouths. These discharge millions of tons of water and sediments annually into the sea[2].

These environmental zones stand out clearly in the Delta region, namely: fresh water swamps, salt water swamps and sandy beaches[3].

Situated on the boundary between the fresh water swamp and the salt water swamp, Iduma territory includes areas belonging to two out of these three zones.

---

2. N. P. Iloeje, A new geography of Nigeria, 1965, page 187
3. Loc. Cit.

The area to the North and North West falls into the fresh water swamp zone. Here, the river water is usually fresh, though sometimes brackish. The land though flooded between August and early October is about 2 feet above water level during the rest of the year. The clayey, reddish brown soil supports the growth of high trees such as Abura, oil palm, raffia palm, mahogany, oboche, iroko, etc. It is suitable for farming.

The area to the South-West and the East falls into the salt water swamp zone. Here, the water is salt-laden and tidal. The soil is black silt and most of the area is low-lying, subject to twice daily flood of a foot or two at high tide. The red mangrove tree constitutes over 98% of the vegetation.

This tree serves some economic purposes; it can be used for pit props, building, cooking and salt making. The salt water environment, though it rules out farming, gives strong encouragement to the fisherman. Iduma then has access to two very different sets of natural resources. Though known to the wider world as Idema, the people call themselves Iduma, a sub-clan within Abureni[4].

The Iduma people are often identified with two other neighbouring communities, Okoroba and Agrisaba as the "Mini" communities. This appellation originated with the Nembe people and all early writers came to follow it. The na me "Mini" is a term which started out as "Nimi" and was corrupted to "Mini" by the early administrators who had difficulties in the pronunciation and writing of the language. "Nimi" in the Nembe language means "wise" and was first applied by Nembe people to Iduma, Okoroba and Agrisaba in particular[5]. These three communities were famous for food production, and anytime they took their foodstuff to their customers at Nembe (Adebe), the Nembe people would take undue advantage, and tried to cheat them by offering low prices,

---

4. Idema is the name of the principal town, while Iduma of the earliest settlement/city, and of the people.
5. John I. Ebifa Adiboko, Circa. 78 years, personal interview @ Idema, on 25/07/2008.

instead of allowing themselves to be cheated, the so called "Nimi" people took their foodstuff home.

As a result of their canny and uncompromising character, they became known all over as "Niminogu" for short "Nimi" meaning wise people and later corrupted to "Mini". However, their wider group or clan identification acknowledged by the people themselves is Abureni[6].

The Abureni clan consists of three sub groups name ly: (i) Kugbo (ii) Iduma and (iii) Okorobo (Emeke).

(i) Kugbo group; comprising, Emago, Amuruto, Akani, Amorokeni, Ebilailagh. Of these, only serial 4 is in Ogbia Local Government Area in Bayelsa State, the rest are in Abua/Odual Local Government Area in Rivers State.

(ii) Iduma group; comprising, Iduma, Idema, Eboh, Obeduma, Oboghe, Oruan (Atubo I), Emalo and the satellite communities. All the communities are in Ogbia Local Government Area, Bayelsa State.

---

6. Ibid.

(iii) Emeke group; comprising, Agrisaba (Obemeke), Okorobo (Edumanom), Ogboma, etc. All the communities are in Nembe LGA, Bayelsa State. In 1991, a government census put the population of Iduma at 12,516[7].

1.3 Community Organization and Architecture

Abureni clan comprised three sub-groups: Iduma, Kugbo (Obo-agbain) and Okorobo (Edumanom).

This work is particularly on Iduma, hence I will be more concerned on the Iduma sub-group in analyzing the way the community is organized and its architecture, as a model.

Idema is one of the main villages in the Iduma-sub-group. There are fourteen (14) lineage groups (Oghol-Otu) and several families (Eghun-Otu) in each of the lineage groups. The community has both a community meeting

---

7. Source: National Population Commission (1997) Census '91 Final Results: Rivers State

hall (Igula) and a central town square (Obetire), all located in separate places. While the central village square is at the centre of the town the community hall is almost at one end of the town.

The town has a major road running through and dividing it into two almost equal halves. From this road, minor roads link the town to the waterside on the side of the Idema creek.

The fourteen lineage groups on which the town is settled constitute the names of the compounds. Relationshi p within the group is based on historical lineage ties either by direct blood link or through marital bond. There are defined boundaries between compounds, and a few open spaces in some of the compounds.

The original house architecture used to be a single linear structure consisting of two or three rooms. One of the rooms served as the sitting (living) room, there was also a detached kitchen where the family cooked and later moved the food to the living room for consumption. The wife and children slept in one of the rooms. The third room was usually reserved for the husband.

There was no provision for bathroom and toilet, as villagers prefer to take their baths, at the waterside, where they also used the public toilets.

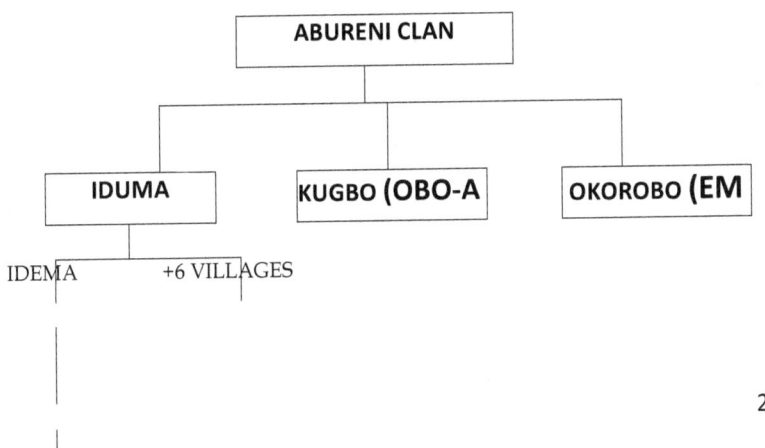

14 "War Canoe HOUSES" (OGHOL-OTU)

SEVERAL FAMILIES (EGHUN-OTU)

INDIVIDUAL HOUSEHOLDS

Figure 1: Structure of Idema in Abureni clan

In early times, houses were built of mud walls and raffia palm roofs (akain). Later the walls were made of burnt bricks. Presently, houses are built of cement blocks and corrugated iron roofing sheets, or special roofing tiles depending on the financial ability of the owner of the property.

1.4 Literature Review

The very few authors that have written about this part of the Niger Delta usually mentioned Idema or "Mini" in passing except one or two cases that have specifically mentioned Iduma. This is evidently due to lack of knowledge on the people.

Some of the early works to have mentioned "Mini" was *The Peoples of Southern Nigeria*, London, 1926, by P.A. Talbot. Here, Talbot classified Mini as a clan within the Western Ijaw sub-tribe. For Idema, one of the earliest documents that mentioned it, was with respect to a declarative judgment delivered on Monday 3rd March, 1913 by His Honour, Mr. Justice A.F.C. Webber of the Supreme Court of the Colony of Southern Protectorate of Nigeria at the Calabar Division, in the case of Chiefs Dick Harry Braide and Others representing the people of Saka, Kugbo and Idema versus Chiefs Allagoa and Egbelu representing the Brass people. Here, the Justice held that the Idemas, Kugbos and Saka (Odual) were independent people who were entitled to their property. He also described the Idemas as the people who occupy the buffer zone between the Kalabaris and the Brass people.

Another early document that made scattered reference to Idema was the "Report on the Historical and Administrative Structure of Nembe" (1932) by E. N. Dickinson. This report pointed out the long-standing connection between the "Mini" communities of Idema, Okoroba and Agrisaba in the North East of Nembe. Nothing more, was said about the Iduma people in that report.

The "Report of the Commission of Inquiry into the Nembe Chieftaincy Dispute", as published in the Eastern Region of Nigeria Government Official Gazette No. 24 of 1960 also mentioned Idema but not Iduma. Here, the Report listed, Okoroba, Idema and Agrisaba as not of Nembe stock, being as they claim but are grouped in the Nembe clan for administrative convenience. In *The Small Brave City State*, a work that was published in 1964, by Professor Ebiegberi Joe Alagoa, Idema was merely mentioned in passing by the process of the author attempting to describe the geographical location of Nembe. He referred to Idema as a distinct town on the periphery, which came within the political sphere of the Brass city state at one time or another.

In a compilation of the Administrative Divisions of Rivers State by E. W. Appah, Esq. Port Harcourt, January, 1969 at page 11, Idema was listed as a principal town in Rivers State.

In another of Professor E. J. Alagoa's books titled *A History of the Niger Delta, I.U.P 1972*; the work provides some details on the MINI – NEMBE relations. Here, he revealed how the ouster Nembe Leader Kala-Ekule staged a political come back with the aid of a Mini migrant Ogio who eventually found his own dynasty in Nembe. Also in this book, he talked of two types of communities that came within the Nembe political sphere, first, those like Okpoma, Twon, and Odioma who shared the langua ge and culture of the metropolis and second, the Mini villages of Idema, Okoroba and Agrisaba who had their own distinctive language and culture. That was all the author talked about Iduma.

In Professor E. J. Alagoa's article on *Ke: The History of an Old Delta Community* in Oduma magazine volume 2 No. 1, 1974. Here, Idema is listed among a number of other towns that traced their founding father from 'Ke' in the Eastern Delta.

Another reference to Idema can be found in E. J. Alagoa's article titled *The Niger Delta States and their Neighbours* in J. F. A. Ajayi and Crowder (ed) 1976, History of West Africa vol. No. 2, page 352. The reference here is to the bravado of Idema as a leading community that participated in the celebrated head-hunting exercise of old.

In Christian Egiri's unpublished thesis titled: *Palm Oil Production and Marketing in the Ogbia and Nembe areas of Rivers State*, University of Port Harcourt, 1983. Egiri lists two palm oil producing camps namely, Ozim-Onyeke and Otuogba that were established within Iduma and operated during the peak of the Atlantic oil trade. His work which deals with Ogbia generally made no further reference of Iduma economic or political life.

My unpublished thesis titled: *An Economic and Political History of Idema from Early Times to Present*, University of Port H arcourt, 1985, is perhaps the first fairly detailed work on Idema. In the work I attempted to present the economic and political life of Idema from early times to 1985. I examined the origin of the Idema people, its social, political and economic settings over times, its relations with its neighbours, the effect of the Nigerian Civil War, the effect of party politics on the people. Unfortunately, the work remained unpublished. From 1985 to present, some important historical events must have taken place which needed to be examined.

In E. E. Efere and Kay Williamson's work on "Languages" in E. J. Alagoa and Tekena N. Tamuno's (eds) *Land and People of Nigeria: Rivers State*, Iduma was listed as one of the communities within the Kugbo-Ogbia language cluster in the Central Delta group. The classification itself is a misnomer and showed lack of proper knowledge of the people whose languages were being studied. The classification ought to be Ogbia-Abureni cluster, Kugbo being a dialect of Abureni.

Perhaps the most recent work where Idema is further mentioned in the usual passing references is in Mark Atei Okorobia's contribution titled: *The Central Niger Delta* in E. J. Alagoa and others (ed), *The Izon of the Niger Delta*, Port Harcourt, 2009, page 483.

Here, Idema was mentioned as one of the Abureni communities where most Bassambiri merchants established marriage alliances done with the intention to protect their interest in the producing communities.

All in all, no previous work on this area has given us a detailed treatment of Iduma general history. The desire for a documented history of the Iduma people has also become overdue. There is also the saying that nobody can tell your story better than you can do. Hence, my attempt at a more penetrating work on the history of the Iduma people in the Niger Delta.

1.5 Sources and Problems:

In this study, traditions of origin, perhaps the most controversial type of oral literature have been used as source material. In a study which attempts to go back as far into the past as sources permit, it is only logical to test what traditions of origin can reveal, with full awareness of their limitations.

Oral tradition was the most extensively used source because it was the most abundant source of historical information in this area.

As a source, oral tradition has its own peculiar problems. The basic limitation of traditions of origin is the chronological. For, although they are cast in the form of accounts of the beginn ing of peoples, they really refer to only a fraction of the history of such peoples. The oral traditions of origin clearly go back less than a thousand years. Secondly, oral traditions, then, do not cover all of the history of any people, but for a people without written history, they take us further back than any available source. Archaeology would be helpful, but no excavations have been done in Iduma.

There is also the problem of chronological difficulty even in the period following the tradition of origin. In some traditional societies a time scale is provided by the passage of successive reigns and dynasties. A simple method of converting such relative chronology to an estimated absolute dating is to work out a mean length of reign from the dated recent portion of King-list, and to apply that mean to the rest of the list. As noted by E. J. Alagoa in a study carried out, the mean of 13 years has been obtained for 71 African dynasties[8].

---

8. Cited in D. H. Jones, "Problems of African chronology" journal of
    African History Vol. XI, No 2, 1970, in E. J. Alagoa, History of the
    Niger Delta, Ibadan, 1972, page 4

I attempted to apply this to Iduma in full realization of the inescapable difficulties in adopting a King-list.

The traditions of origin are interpreted with the understanding that they refer to only founders of dynasties or of the propriety groups of settlements. Even the most casual study of any of the sub-groups or lineages within such communities remembers variant traditions of origin.

This factor played out prominently in Obeduma history, where two variant traditions of origin of the Awo lineage were recounted.

As a source, oral tradition has its own peculiar problems, which I tried to take account of in my use of it.

Firstly, I ensured that my sources of information were also drawn from other communities such as Ke and Nembe that featured in the Iduma traditions. Secondly, in addition to listening to the narratives given, at the end of every narration, I asked questions for a better understanding of the issues involved.

To supplement my notes, I employed tapes in recording some of my interviews. Although there were initial resentments by the older folks who were not familiar with this method, but this was eventually overcome by explanation as to the reasons for the use of tapes.

Other source material used includes written records, linguistic and ethnographic data. The paucity of written records covering the early period of this study notwithstanding, there were some documents in the form of court judgments, church records, family diaries, personal diaries, administrative reports and even intelligent reports which served as useful primary sources for this work.

However, a variety of non-narrative sources were also used particularly in evaluating the indications of the traditions of origin.

CHAPTER 2
ORIGIN, MIGRATION AND SETTLEMENT

The Traditions

There are three variant versions of the traditions of origin of Iduma. The first tradition is largely held by the Idema (Aye) and Eboh major lineages or sub-groups of Iduma, while the other two traditions are held by the Opuso and Awo lineages or sub-groups of Obeduma Community.

These versions have come about in recent times as a result of the political rivalries plaguing the two major lineages that make up Obeduma - namely Opuso and Awo - in their various claims to royalty and parcels of land within Obeduma jurisdiction.

2.1(i) The Idema (Aye)/Eboh Version

This tradition claims that a man called "Omongi", though known to the Ke people as

Omoye[1] and his younger brother Fenibo fled from Ke, a community in the Eastern part of the Niger Delta. They fled from the community with their wives and children on account of an outbreak of a strange deadly disease, which had claimed several lives in the community. The strange disease was suspected to be an epidemic.[2]

Upon leaving Ke they moved westwards, and settled first at "Okoma"[3.] From Okoma they moved on and later settled at another place which came to be known as Idumanamugbo. It was at Idumanamugbo that Omongi's wife who was then pregnant, went into labour

---

1. Informants were:

i. HRH Felix E.A Igoniwari, J.P Olilaema of Idema, 44 years @ Idema on tape UPH/A on 7/4/85

ii. Chief Ngogo Owitubo, 75 years @ Ke, 8/9/84

iii. S.B Ngogo, 72 years @ Ke, 8/9/84

iv. Nwoke .D. Agbani, 70 years, @ Ke 8/9/84, 5. S.O Benibo circa 70 years @ Ke 8/9/84

2. See E.J. Alagoa Ke "The History of an Old Delta Community" in Oduma magazine, vol.2 No.1 Aug , 1974 at page 7

3. Okoma is the name of the island close to the present Kula community where Omongi first settled, upon leaving "Ke" and successfully gave birth to Iduma. The birth ceremony of Id uma was celebrated at the new settlement, a fact that prompted Omongi to name their settlement after the birth ceremony of Id uma meaning "Idumanamugbo". The name of this place has re mained so, till date.

The event itself brought joy to them and signalled a maj or milestone in their sojourn. Omongi and the remaining memb ers were said to have settled there for a while, before they reloc ated after Omongi's death. Two factors accounted for their relo cation. First was the need for a more secure place of abode, and second was the desire for a more expansive place to practice agr iculture for their sustenance. In their bid to achieve these compelling needs, Iduma who was then grown, discovered the present site of Iduma where he and the other members finally settled. Hence the settlement was named after him as the principal founder. Fenibo who was then very old, was said to have died a few years later.

Iduma had three sons: Aye, Eboh and Obe. Aye succeeded his father (Iduma) as King of the settlement after his father's death. Aye begat Igoniwari and Ebo. Igoniwari begat Obodiri, Ogu, Ikoni, and Ikpoku; while Ebo begat Adiboko and Eme.

The tradition maintains that Eboh begat Ologo, lvi, Akariosu, Ibem, Obodom and Agadi. Though some informants claim that Agadi was not a direct son of Eboh but of Amorokeni descent and came to live with Ologo, having first settled at Edumarugbe (Emata-Agadi) near the Kugbo Bay[4]. And Obe begat Opuso. The Opuso lineage in Obeduma is said to be the royal family that produces the Olilaema of Obeduma[5]. Fenibo begat Eghunuma, and Eghunuma begat Edegele, Ataki and Okoto. Edegele begat Obolom (Obulom), while Ataki begat Ekpo[6]. During the reign of King Aye, the Iduma settlement became a target of incessant attacks by enemies

4. Informants were: Capt Glory Koru, (rtd.) circa. 70 years, Idema, 27/10/16, 2. Chief I.L Ivi, circa 76 years Eboh 2/08/2016.
5. Simeon M. A. Opuso, 42 years, personal interview, Obeduma, 8/4/1985
6. Johnny J. Eghunuma, 42 years, personal interview, Idema, 6/9/84

mostly from Nembe area. In order to avoid further attacks, King Igoniwari, upon assumption of office as Olilaema, proposed a relocation of the community to a site directly on the opposite bank of the Iduma creek.

Before the relocation, King Igoniwari sent for a medicine man called Okiki, a native of Ayun in the Odual area, for the cleansing of the proposed site, which had hitherto been used for disposing the dead. Okiki came with an assistant called Osoko for the assignment. When they had performed the cleansing rites, King Igoniwari was still not prepared to move into the new settlement, until Okiki and his men had slept there for seven (7) Ake days (28 days) without being hurt before he finally moved in. When King Igoniwari had settled in, Eboh and Obe later moved over to join him. They settled at two strategic locations. Eboh settled at the East flank and Obe at the West, to ward off enemies from any of the directions. The movement of Igoniwari to the new settlement as king marked the dawn of a new dynasty which became known as the Igoniwari dynasty, in Iduma history; and henceforth became the main royal lineage in Idema (Aye).

For the services rendered by Okiki, he was compensated with the honour of sitting by the main door on the platform of the town meeting house (Igula), where all the lineage heads sit. Again, in the event of any sacrifice, Okiki was to always eat the neck of the sacrificial meat.

This version also claims that a civil war, resulting from dissatisfaction over the sharing of pepper soup prepared with sacrificial meat during a festival occurred no sooner than Igoniwari took over as the Olilaema (King) of Iduma, with Ebo as his deputy. Consequently, Ibem and Obodom who were members of Eboh lineage moved out of Iduma and proceeded to Agholo (Kolo).

They arrived Kolo at a period when their host's settlement was in great distress of an epidemic threatening to wipe out the entire settlement. Ibem was approached by Agholo to save his people from extinction due to the calamity. Ibem being a man imbued with great magical powers was able to save the Agholo people from the calamity. Ibem and Obodom later lived amongst the Kolo people. This event thus created brotherly ties betwee n Iduma and Agholo (Kolo) that culminated to exchange of visits over the years.

Following the same event of dissatisfaction over the pepper soup meat, another group comprising Ekpo, and Obolom (Obulom), of the Fenibo lineage also moved out of the settlement. While Ekpo settled a few metres away from Oruama (Eghunuma old settlement), Obolom (Obulom) proceeded to Ogonokom in Abua area where he settled briefly upon leaving Iduma. He later moved out of Ogonokom and settled at Obomuotu, and later at Okeinodu. It was from Okeinodo that he finally proceeded and founded Obolom (Obulom) or Abulomini. The name Abulomini was later corrupted by the early colonial administrators to Abuloma[7].

---

7. Informants were: (1) HRH F.E.A. Igoniwari, JP Olilaema 43 years, at Idema
7th April 1985 on tape No UPH/A, (2) Chief Isu Otolo Oga Circa . 102 years, at Idema, 12/08/84, (3) Chief Ibitamuno L.E Obodiri, 44 years, Idema 6/9/84

The Abuloma people are presently located amongst the Okrika-Ijaws in Port Harcourt Local Government Area, in Rivers State. The Abuloma people speak a language similar to Abureni and Ogbia spoken by the Iduma people.

This version further maintains that Eghunuma lived at his Oruama abode for a long while where he also played the role of an informant to the main settlement in the event of any external invaders before relocating to the new settlement. Eghunuma's late coming to the main settlement accounted for the lineage not having much residential land at Idema.

In recognition of the role of his father as co-founder of Iduma, he was accorded the honour of cracking the head of any person, elected as Olilaema of Iduma. This version further maintains that Eghunuma does not have any blood ties with the Awo lineage of Obeduma.

2.1(ii) The Opuso Version

The tradition follows the first one up to the point where Obe moved out of Iduma and found his new settlement or community at Igbain-Obeduma (Obeduma old site). This version claims Obe moved away from his brothers Aye and Eboh to settle at this new settlement in order to guard against enemies from that direction from harming inhabitants of their first settlement.

It also claims that Obe was later approached by a man called Awo, a stranger of Ijo descent with a request that he be all owed to live among those children of Iduma in Obe's settlement. When Obe finally granted Awo's request, he later did not come in person to settle with Obe but sent some of his children namely, Obeten and Agiakoro, who initially settled, but left and dwelt with Eghunuma at Oruama. While at Oruama, Awo's children wronged their host and were consequently driven out.

Having been driven out of Oruama, Awo and his lineage then turned back to Igbain-Obeduma where they were later allowed to settle. On a certain Ake day (resting day) when the villagers were gathered and palm wine was being served, a disagreement arose between the children of Obe and those of Awo. Akani, a granddaughter of Obe, intercepted a cup of palm wine (a min-ide) that was being served to Obeten, with the reason that Anikrika, an elder, ought to have been served before Obeten who was junior to him. The seizure of the palm wine from Obeten's hand was considered an insult by the other children of Awo, who later moved out of the community.

This tradition maintains that Obe's children, including Opuso, who was then the head of the community (Olilaema), continued to live there until one Abu, fleeing from Nembe menance, arrived with other immigrants from Ayun-Amorokoin.

Some years later when Ekere from the Opuso lineage became the head of the community, he relocated to the present Obeduma site, which is just a few metres from the old site. Here, he was approached by Awo and his lineage with a request that they might join up again with the children of Obe. Notwithstanding their past differences the tradition maintained, Ekere decided to accommodate them, and they have lived together ever since[8].

2.1(iii) The Awo Version

In this version, Omongi is said to have moved from Ke to Ibasa and then to Idumanamugbo before settling at Iduma. This tradition maintains that Omongi had two sons namely, Iduma and Fenibo. Iduma begat Aye, Eboh and Obe, while Fenibo begat Eghunuma and Awo. When the group settled at Iduma the place was still unsafe for them for reasons that Nembe invaders often sneaked in from behind the settlement to kill people at night.

To guard against such occurrence, Igoniwari, a son to Aye, on becoming King (Olilaema), sought for the

---

8. Informants were:

i. HRH Simeon M. A. Opuso Olilaema of Obeduma, 42 years @

Obeduma, 8th April, 1985, on tape No UPH/A

ii. Chief Isu Otolo Oga, circa 102 years, Idema, 12/8/84

services of a medicine man called Okiki, a native of Ayun in Odual to cleanse a site on the opposite bank of the river which was then a burial ground, for relocation. After the medicine man had purified the new site, King Igoniwari ordered that the medicine man (Okiki) should first stay there for a while and if nothing happens to anybody before he would relocate. Okiki and his group obeyed and accordingly slept in the new site for seven Ake days, (28 days) without harm before King Igoniwari finally relocated, with his people.

In the process of getting them settled, King Igoniwari occupied the middle land, while Eboh took the right flank and Obe the left flank in a way strategically designed to check enemy encroachment.

At the same time, Awo passed beyond Obe's settlement and settled at a place which came to be known as Obekotawo, while Eghunuma founded a new community called Oruama.

While Awo was at Obekotawo, Opuso the eldest son of Obe later approached him in order to make use of part of his land which was then unsettled. Awo acceded to Opuso's request, and Opuso settled at the site which later came to be known as Obeduma. In due course, when Ekere was installed as the Olila ema of Obeduma, Arugu Egbedum, a direct son of Awo was ab le to put up the first building at the present Obeduma site, and was later joined by other descendants of Awo and Opuso respe ctively[9].

2.2 A Critical Appraisal of the Traditions

In our appraisal of the traditions of origin, let us follow t he order of their narration, and start with the assertion that the ancestor of the Iduma people came from the Kalabari speaking community of Ke. How convincing is this myth of origin? In the oral tradition or history of a community, it is common to find myths which trace its origin to a community considered autocht honous or politically superior, and which reflect not the facts of

---

9. Orlu Samuel, c. 72 years, personal interview at Obeduma 5th April

    1985 on tape No UPH/B

history but the desire for prestige. Could this be one of such my ths? In order to answer this question, I shall look both at the ora l tradition of Ke itself, and at the linguistic and cultural evidenc

e. At first glance, the linguistic evidence flatly contradicts that of both the Iduma and Ke traditions. Thus, while Iduma speaks Abureni, a language which, with the neighbouring Ogbia, Abua and Odual, belongs to the Central Delta sub-branch of the Delta cross family of Niger–Congo, the Ke speak Kalabari, an Eastern Ijo language which belongs to the Ijoid family of Niger-Congo [10]. The absence of any close linguistic affinity seems to rule out any idea of common origin for the two communities.

However, traditions collected at Ke confirm the Iduma traditions with the claim to Ke. Generally, there seemed not to be great divergence from these traditions, since the cause of the migration is attributed to an

---

10. Kay Williamson, "The linguistic evidence for the pre history of the
    Niger Delta" in E.J. Alagoa, F.N. Anozie, and Nwanaa Nzewunwa, eds.
    The early history of the Niger Delta, Hamburg, (1988), page 24

epidemic (si obi) from both sources. And again, both sources are in agreement with the names of the ancestral fathers that moved out of Ke, except the name of Omongi which the Ke tradition maintain to be Omoye.

Turning from linguistic to socio-cultural evidence, we seem once more to find corroboration of the oral tradition. First of all when we look at Iduma we find that rights over children are vested in the mother's side. This matrilineal system seems to set Iduma apart from the other villages in the Abureni group from neighbouring Ogbia, Abua and Odual and links her to the Kalabari speaking area.

Although, it could also be argued that the matrilineal system of inheritance could have been brought about as a result of influence of Nembe culture on Iduma in later years as the community developed.

There are, in fact a number of other cultural traits which set Iduma apart from her Ogbia neighbours and link her with kalabari. Thus institutions such as the Ekine Society (Sekiapu) and masquerade displays are very common with Iduma, while they are conspicuously absent in most of the Ogbia towns/villages.

In Iduma one observes that up to about three (3) decades ago, most of the singing and dancing associated with water-spirits (kuku music) and social clubs was done in Kalabari-ijo. Again, during most social functions, for instance, in times of wrestling contests, the drum-names of individuals are cast and beaten in Kalabari-Ijo by the talking drum (Ogbuzu). The drum praise, for the spirit of the community (enai-ema)[11] is still beaten in Kalabari-Ijo.

It is: *"Obo Iduma gbori bio gbori bio*
"Obo Iduma gbori bio gbori bio
Toru Paka Ikio fa"
Meaning
"Great Iduma bound
in one mind and unity does not
know friend once on the river"

---

11. "Enai-ema" Is a spirit of the community. Just like every individual has a guiding spirit so is the belief that every community is inbued with a spirit, on whom libation and invocation is made.

The wording of the drum praise as we can observe are all cast in Kalabari-ijo with exception of only two words "obo Iduma" meaning "Great Iduma" which is in a language similar to Ogbia.

The names of the early settlers and in fact most names contained in the King-list of the Iduma tradition, Omongi, Fenibo, Iduma, Aye Igoniwari, Opuso, Aloki, Osomu, Ene, Ikuli sound more like Kalabari-Ijo names than names derived from Ogbia or even Nembe who are their closest neighbours. In short the socio-cultural evidence seems to give strong support to the traditions of origin, both as recorded at Iduma and as comfirmed at Ke.

At this point we may look for a hypothesis which can explain the conflict between the narratives and socio-cultural evidence on the one hand and the linquistic evidence on the other. The most plausible hypothesis would seem to be that the early settlers were indeed Kalabari-ijo speakers from Ke, but that, some time after their arrival at their present sites, they underwent a language shift[12]; such a shift would have taken place had the migrants settled at a site already heavily populated through a change-over to the language of the aborigines.

However, since the tradition says nothing about any such aborigines, this seems unlikely. What seems more likely is that the shift was the result of people and influences coming in after the initial settlement. Thus Okiki, a medicine man from Odual is mentioned by all the traditions as the person who performed the purification rites which enabled the migrants to build up th eir new settlement. Okiki was said to have come to Iduma with an assistant called Osoko. Okiki and Osoko who later relocated to Iduma with their lineage groups are the great

---

12. "Language shift" is a process whereby speakers of one lan guage
    abandon their language in favour of another which norm ally takes at
    least two generations

progenitors of the Okikiayun and Osoko group of Houses in Id uma. Up to present, the Okikiayun lineage or sub-group remain s one of the largest in Iduma.

    Again, the Abu lineage is also mentioned by most of the traditions as immigrants from Ayun-Amorokoin who came and settled with the Awo group at Obeduma.

    The decline of the Ebela Kingdom, and Amirowel which were contiguous communities to Iduma may have also produc ed immigrants who sought shelter with Iduma. Both Ebela and Amiriowel were known to be heavily populated, at the time. Al l these factors must have contributed to bringing about language shift in Iduma giving rise to the Abureni language which is a mixture of Kalabari-ijo, Ogbia and Odual[13].

In the latter portions of the traditions of origin, one finds a close affinity between the Aye/Eboh and Opuso versions and a number of striking differences between

---

13. "Abureni Language" comprised Kalabari-Ijo, Odual and Ogbia forms,
    thus Iduma people reasonably understand and can communicate in
    each of these languages.

these two and the Awo version. Thus, with respect to both the initial places of settlement and to the genealogies of the early settlers, there is unity of opinion between the Aye/Eboh and the Opuso traditions. Thus, both maintain that Omongi briefly settled at Okoma and that it was at Idumanamugbo that Iduma was born. Both also claim that Omongi begat Iduma, while Iduma begat three sons, Aye, Eboh, and Obe. Also, that Fenibo the brother of Omongi begat Eghunuma, while Obe begat Opuso. This means in essence that Awo has no relationship with either of the other two groups i.e Aye/Eboh and Opuso. The proponents of t he Awo tradition by contrast claim that Omongi begat Fenibo and Iduma, and Fenibo begat Eghunuma and Awo, and Iduma begat Aye, Eboh and Obe. Both sets of traditions seem to be consistent in their various claims, and it is difficult to choose between them in respect of authenticity.

The issue of early settlers at Obeduma and of who owned the Obeduma land is scarcely touched on, in the Aye/Eboh version, but is central to the Opuso and Awo versions. The two, however, are in complete disagreement on this matter.

Judging on how both sets serve to authenticate present-day political and economic claims as expressed on Awo's quest for equality with Opuso within the political realm in respect of the administration of Obeduma, and the right on the ownership of the disputed Obeduma land. Hence it becomes difficult to choose between both in respect of authenticity. Thus, both traditions seem to be products of politically motivated distortions from the Aye/Eboh tradition, which appear most convincing of them all.

2.3 Chronology

Arriving at a date for the founding of Iduma is obviously a difficult task, since there are no written records referring to the early period and giving absolute dates and no archaeological data. However, oral traditions collected from Nembe, Ke and I duma have been very emphatic in recognising Iduma as a community of great antiquity.

Tradition at Iduma also reveals a list of kings numbering sixteen, who had so far ruled Iduma from the time of migration up to the present. These Kings are named as follows: Omongi, Fenibo, Iduma, Aye, Igoniwari, Obodiri, Ogu, Ikoni, Ikpoku, Ene, Osomu, Aloki, Otolo, Ikuli (died 1929), Abiosi (died 1963), Felix (installed 1974); see appendixes II & III.

At first glance, the absence of recorded absolute dates for the reigns of three or four of the more recent kings makes it impossible for us to use the mean start-to-start of reign method, which establishes an average figure for reign-plus-interregnum for recent kings and then extrapolate backwards.

However, turning once to the oral traditions collected at Iduma and Nembe, Aloki the 12th King on the Iduma King-list is mentioned to be a contemporary with King Mein of Bassambiri-Nembe. If Aloki was a contemporary to Mein, and the latter can be dated 1800-1832 since he was a contemporary to King Forday Kulo of Ogbolomabiri-

Nembe[14], it then means that a tentative date can also be worked out for the chronology of the reigns of the sixteen (16) kings that had ruled Iduma. If this is accepted, it means there have been t hree completed reigns plus interregnum in the last 142 years, from 1832-1974. This gives a mean figure for reign plus interregnum of 47 years. Extrapolating backwards from 1974 on the basis of this figure we get 47 × 15 = 705 or roughly 700 years and (subtracting 700 from 2017) gives *circa* 1317 for the founding of Iduma Community.

However, recognising the circacumstances of the pitfalls of this method is very important, and once it is taken care of, I believe tentative dates such as the above is tenable.

---

14. E.J. Alagoa, The Small Brave City state, (1964), P.83

CHAPTER 3

ECONOMIC ORGANIZATION IN THE PRE-COLONIAL ERA

In this chapter I shall try to outline the economic organization of Iduma in the pre-colonial era. The basis for my outline will be what the custodians of oral tradition consider to be the " age old" features of Iduma economy.

3.1   Land Tenure and farming

In Iduma, the limited supply of arable land for agricultural activities made necessary a land tenure system: i.e a system of rules for the orderly allocation of land to individuals and lineage groups.

Two types of land were available to the people for farming. One was called okukwa – land on the river banks and quite close to the village/town. This land was comparatively small in total area, permanently held by individuals and could be passed to the sister's children or other maternal relations if the holder died. The other types of farmland were eghana and ikpu – land found in the depths of forest. The difference between eghana and ikpu lies only on the frequency of usage. Eghana is one which has not been cultivated for a longer duration (from 4 years and above) while ikpu is one in which its frequency of use or cultivation is from 2 – 4 years.

Such land was relatively large in total area, and was held in trust by the House Head (Olila-Otu), who apportioned it o ut to members of his "House" at the beginning of every farming season and it reverts to "House" ownership at the end of the season[1].

Farming was an important economic activity and it was mostly done by the women most times in plantation settlements outside the towns/villages on the ikpu farmlands. Several plantations either owned by individuals or lineages were scattered around at both

---

1. The term "House" is reference to a sociopolitical unit made up of individuals who claim descent through the female line to a common ancestor who is the founder of the house, and sometimes gives his name to it.

nearby and far away settlements. Some of these, were as follows: Oruan (Atubo I), Obhietia (Obiata), Asaga (Agada), Edumarugbe (Ematagadi), Oboagbugbo, Oboatobi, Iwurade, Adigiasikolo, etc.

Clearing of the bush was done between the months of September and November, against the planting season which starts usually from late November to early April. The annual flood had left behind its enriching deposit of silt, and there was still enough moisture in the soil to promote plant growth.

On the okukwa, mounds were made, and crops such as cassava, cocoyam, melon, maize, sugarcane, water yam, pepper and other vegetables were grown. On the ikpu additional crops such as plantain, banana, and different species of cocoyam were planted. The trees were felled to allow in enough sunlight to enable the planted crops grow well.

During the months of April and May, farmers, harvested those of the earlier planted crops, such as maize, cassava, and vegetables, which required a shorter time to mature. While weeding the farms at this time of the year, farmers and their families fed on these harvested crops in anticipation of the time they would harvest the staples such as the cocoyam, plantain, banana, etc, by August.

The various implements used by the farmers include: the African hoe (esuwa), matchet (ogidi), and axe (akubu).

Throughout the farming period, the family comprised of the husband, wives, the unmarried children, and the sisters children who served as the production unit.

The husband obtained ikpu land from his maternal house-head or begged from neighbours for the wife and children to farm on. When the bush had been cleared, he planted the plantain and banana suckers and fell the trees after all the crops had been planted. Except for the rare cases in which he himself was a professional farmer, the husband returned after this to his own occupation, leaving his wife and his unmarried children to carry out all other necessary farming operations.

Sometimes, the children of the community constituted themselves into age-group farming teams or work-parties which cut across individual lineages. They exchanged services on specific days and at the end of each day, food was prepared by the host and all were entertained. This system was geared towards co-operation in the various plantations and also to ensure greater productivity.

Surpluses of crops such as cocoyam, plantain, banana, sugar-cane, maize, etc were sold to customers from Nembe, Kalabari and Okrika who visited the various plantations where Iduma people settlerd.

In order to avoid the rotting of surpluses during years of bumper harvest, the producers personally took these crops to their various customers and exchanged them for salt, sea foods etc[2].

3.2 Palm Oil/Kernel Production

Apart from farming which was predominantly done by the women folk, there was also palm oil and kernel production, in which the fruits were gathered by the men, and processed by both men and women. Palm cutting was done by the men on all types of land, where the oil palm tree was available, since Iduma land tenure laws did not restrict the palm-cutter to his own land. It was mostly done during the dry season when the trees were less slippery to climb. In the rainy season those who knew only palm cutting continued with it while those with more than one occupation took to another trade until the next dry season.

Two types of oil involving different methods of processing were produced at the time. The first type was known as oku nu, and was used for domestic purposes. When he wanted to start production, a man spent two to

---

2. Informants were:
   i. Madam Ikokosi Ogumade Circa. 85 years @ Eboh 10/8/84

   ii. Madam Elizabeth Offor Daniel, Circa. 45 years, Idema, 21/8/84.

three days gathering fresh palm fruits. He then called on his wives, children and relations to remove the berries from the stalks. The fruits were boiled in a clay pot and later turned into an ok porogum (unwidened canoe), where the palm fruits were poun ded with leg. The pounded fruits were then transferred into a canoe half filled with water at the water front, and the raw oil separated from the fibre and kernels by squeezing the oil out of the fibre. The raw oil was then cooked again for several hours to produce soft palm-oil.

At this stage, the palm kernel which has been separated from the fibres were taken out from the canoe half filled with water and later dried in the sun for some days and bagged for sale. The kernels were sometimes used locally for the production of liquid cream, oil etc.

Large scale production was carried out by the men to produce a certain type of oil known as okemegha amunu, that is "hard oil". This method of production entailed the collection of a large quantity of palm fruits which could take the men some weeks to gather.

The palm fruits were dried on a shelf above the kitchen fire and later put into an old canoe and soaked with water for some hours. The soaked palm fruits were then removed, put into a very long canoe and covered with plantain and cocoyam leaves. They were kept in this long canoe for at least three days for fermentation and natural heating up.

On the fourth day, the palm fruits were then transferred from the canoe into an Okporogum (unwidened canoe) where t hey were pounded along with some cooked fresh palm fruits with legs and the hands supported with sticks.

After it has been properly pounded two to three itita (fences) were spread on the pounded fruits and a long pole placed on it with a rope fastened to both ends of the okporogum (unwidened canoe). Half paddles and clean sticks were immediately employed in turning the pounded fruits until such a time that the pole was pulled off. This then created a gully in the centre of the canoe, exposing part of the raw oil which was collected into containers. The remaining one mixed up with the fibres was later turned into other small canoes each half-filled with water for the oil to be squeezed out of the fibre. Thereafter, it was boiled for a few minutes and cooked later to produce the refined oil.

Oil so produced was also used locally for cooking, as po made and for lighting. However, most of it was sold to outsiders who used them for various purposes.

In the first stage of this process, the wife of the man and some close relations undertook to remove the palm fruits from the sliced bunches, for the next stage, the man called upon a work-party whose composition cut across family and lineage boundaries. Thus, he called on his fellow palm cutters from all sections of the community to come and pound the fruits with him. Th e palm cutter was also expected to reciprocate whenever it was another man's turn in the exercise[3].

---

3. Informants were:
   i.   Chief Isu Otolo Oga, Circa. 102 years @ Idema on 12/8/84.
   ii. Mr. Ekine Apollo, 43 years @ Idema on 15/8/84,
   iii. Sunday Joel, 56 years @ Idema on 15/8/84.

3.3 Raffia Products

Both sexes in Iduma engaged in sophisticated weaving using the raffia trees as a raw material.

(a) **Thatch (akain):** which was used to make the roofs of their houses was locally produced by both men and women from the raffia by weaving. The method used was one in which the hard outer bark was taken off from the leaf mid ribs (soft part of the frond). This hard bark was then sliced into smaller pieces measuring between 3 – 4 feet iseleguma. While some of the iseleguma were allowed to remain in that size, others were further sliced and from them small pieces called ikpisikpisi was produced. Both the iseleguma and ikpisikpisi were used for weaving the leaves of the raffia to produce the thatch.

Thatch making was normally carried out by the individual although at times one or two friends or relations assisted the man in the process of weaving[4].

4. Akio Johnson circa 65 years personal Interview @ Idema on 8/8/84

(b) **Mat making:** On their part, women produced mats of various sizes from raw materials provided by the raffia tree. Mat-making was done mostly in the rainy season when the women were less busy with their farming activities. Mats were produced by the slicing the leaf mid ribs after the outer bark had been taken off. The sliced mid-ribs were then allowed to dry either in the sun or in the kitchen. The dried leaf mid-ribs were then woven with dried screw pine onunu or a species of a bush rope ik oloman[5].

(c) **Fishing Fence (Itita):** Women also made fishing fences – itita, of various sizes out of materials from the same source. They sliced the hard outer bark into small pieces and dried these in the sun or in the kitchen. When the pieces were dry they wove them in the kitchen. They wove them together with ibarabar, a type of bush rope.

5. Informants were:

i. Madam Mammy Johnson, Circa. 68 years, @ Idema, 6/7/94
   ii. Madam Victoria Offor, Circa 52 years, @ Idema, 6/7/94

Yet again, women also made baskets and a type of fishing trap called egheleghel from this same raffia. To produce baskets, they wove together long thin strips of the hard outer bark with ipoke – sliced ropes produced from the young raffia fronds.

This whole range of crafts are produced on an individual basis, and most items were locally used. The surplus, however, were sold within Iduma, and largely to Nembe, Kalabari and Okrika neighbours, in whose territories the raffia palm did not grow[6].

3.4   Canoe/Paddle Production:

The availability of some special strong trees within the fresh water zone made the building of canoes possible. Dug-out canoes were made from the following species –

---

6. Informants were:
   i. Madam Victoria Offor, circa 52 years @ Idema, 13/8/94;
   ii. Madam Elizabeth Offor Daniel, Circa. 53 years @ Idema, 2/8/90

cophira alata obhom, mamea Africana ire, mitragyna ciliate ibh ogh, i.e. abura, nauches diderrichis opepe, chlorophore excelsa i.e. iroko osa[7].

Canoe carving was undertaken by men. To make a canoe, the tree was first felled and cut into an appropriate length depending on the size of the tree. It was then hollowed with adze and axe, since it is narrow and not very regular in shape.

Having completed the initial operation, the carver called in the helpers for this next stage of the work, which involved firing the canoe with dead raffia fronds in order to spread its sides. Aside from canoes, paddles were also produced from these species of trees.

The canoe industry played a significant role in the lives of the people. This was because the canoe and paddle were the basic means of communication in the creeks. As

---

7. Mr. I. J. Abigo, circa 57 years, Asst. Chf. Conservator of forest,
   Rivers State Ministry of Agriculture Natural Resources, Port Harcourt, personal interview on 4/8/84.

an informant reminded me, the canoe and paddle were the tools on which all the other economic activities depended, since it was the means by which people both visited their farms and also carried out fishing in the creeks[8].

Although most of the canoes and paddles produced in Iduma were used by the people themselves, the surpluses were sold, either to neighbouring communities or to more distant people like the Kalabaris and Okrikans.

It is important to note that apart from canoe and paddle production, there were other crafts that were produced by specialized craftsmen from woods. These include motar (ekpa), pistle (edum), steering spoon (ago), etc.

3.5 Hunting

Hunting was practiced on the vast forests around the towns/villages and beyond to neigbhbouring villages.

---

8. Informants were:
   i. Chief Isu Otolo Oga, circa 102 years at Idema, 12/8/84;
   ii. Mr. Lionel Joel Edumologbo, circa 65 years, at Idema, 11/8/84

Spears, matchets, sticks and other locally produced materials were employed in killing animals. A team of hunters could surround a thick bush to comb out animals which were then killed with the matchets. At other times such methods as digging of pit-traps were used to entrap animals which were later killed with spears. The game killed includes, monkeys, bush cats, bush pigs, antelopes, rats and different species of birds.

As an informant told me; when especially big animals such as the elephant or gorilla were killed, certain rites were performed for them, and the meat was not limited to the hunter and his family but shared by the entire community[9].

Apart from wild games that were hunted, snails were also hunted in the forest. Most of it was consumed locally, and the surpluses sold to the Kalabari, Nembe and other ethnic nationalities.

---

9. Marian Daniel, circa 60 years, personal interview @ Idema, 7/8/84

3.6 Fishing

The numerous rivers, creeks and forest ponds encourage both men and women to be actively engaged in fishing throughout the year.

The men engaged themselves in open river fishing in the salt water zone during the rainy season, and retired to baling of ponds in the fresh water forest from November to March of every year.

In the open river fishing, two or three men combined to constitute themselves into a fishing team, and might leave the village for a nearby fishing-port for a period of 7 – 14 days. Their fishing equipments include: fishing fence (itita), which was used to block small creeks and water passages at high tide so that by low tide many fish become trapped. The catch usually includes tilapia (ewala), mullet (obhorom), school master (osisi), golden fish (epelia), lobster (ogiga), etc.

At the end of the dry season, men also dug ponds in the fresh water area for fish to collect during the flood period; such ponds might be dug either deep in the forest or near the river banks. During the next dry season, between the months of November and March, a work group ranging from two to sixty men baled these ponds. The preparation and baling of a small pond owned by an individual needed a work-group of only two or three people. A larger family or lineage pond for instance Atabakoko belonging to the Ebutu lineage in Iduma, was normally baled every ten years with a work group of over sixty men. Different species of fish such as mud fish (obolo), clarias lazera (oborh), xenomystus (ebebelem), and of animals as water turtles (ibor), and crocodile (obaghagha), were caught. The crocodiles were caught using a cane rope called ipoki as a bait.

The animal could bite at the rope and get its jaws hooked, where upon it became helpless. The bait rope was then used to tie its mouth and feet.

Iduma women collected perinwinkles (isam), and oyster (igbain), in the salt water swamp at all times of the year. In addition, they occupied themselves with lake fishing at the peak of the rainy season, using conically shaped trap (egheleghel) made from raffia tree. These, they dropped at strategic places in the lakes with bait of palm fruits. As the fish went into collect-the bait, they automatically got entrapped. The catch include: fresh water crab (adikoro), snake-fish (ogelogel), mud fish (obolo), claries lazera (oborh), and xenomystus (ebebelem)[10].

Most of the fish caught on both the fresh water swamp and the salt water swamp were locally consumed. Surpluses, however, were sold to neighbouring communities such as Odual and Kugbo who are predominantly farmers, compared to the Iduma people.

3.7 Trading

As we have already seen, Iduma people produced surpluses of forest derived goods which were exchanged

10.   i.   Mr. Ebimawoto Daniel, circa. 55 years, @ Idema, 21/3/85;

       ii.   Godspower Johnson, circa 61 years, Idema, 22/8/84;

      iii.   Dr. Oyetayo, of the Dept. of Zoology, University of Port Harcourt, supplied the biological names for the fishes species, 6/2/85, information obtained by personal interview on serial nos. 1-3.

with people of the salt water zone. Iduma people also from time to time produced smaller surpluses of salt water products such as dried/smoked fish, which they exchanged with the Kugbo and Odual people who lived further inside the fresh water zone.

In return for these commodities, they received salt from the Nembe, Akassa, Kalabari and Okrika people, and foodstuffs such as plantain, banana, and cocoyam from the Odual and Kugbo people in times of bad harvest.

Although much of this trade was by barter, several kinds of currency were also in use. Amongst them were the manilla Okpoki Iduma, and the cowrie shell (okoba), were also used as medium of exchange. During the period, there were no specialized traders but the producers traded with their own products[11].

11. Okoni Odu-Eme, circa, 98 years, personal interview @ Idema, 12/8/78

CHAPTER 4

SOCIO-POLITICAL ORGANIZATION IN THE PRE-COLONIAL ERA (1400 – 1800AD)

In the preceding chapter, I examined the economic set up and how it was organized during the pre-colonial era. Having done so, I will now examine the social and political organizations during the period. The family (eghun-otu), "house" (oghol-otu), and the community (ema), were the basic units in this regard. The interplay of each of these units in the socio-political life of Iduma will also be discussed in this chapter.

4.1 The Family (Eghun-Otu)

The husband, wives his children and those of his sisters were the composition of the family, and inheritance was based on maternal line. At the head of each family was a family head, often the oldest man who co-ordinated the affairs of the family.

The family was an important social unit, hence in times of great distress or even prosperity the family was never omitte d in consultation. When a member of the family was seriously ill, it was the closest relations of the family, and the family head that decided what type of treatment was appropriate; and every member of the family made it a point of duty to visit the sick. If at the worst a member of the family died, the family head ensured that all was done to bury the corpse as custom and tradition demands.

If any of the female members of the family wished to marry, they first consulted their parents, and then later consulted the head of the family, whose consent was necessary before a valid marriage could take place. Again, if a member of the family had become indebted to an outsider or had committed any serious crime, for instance murder, it was the head of the family that served as an arbiter to decide who in the family could be pawned out to either defray the debt or act as a substitute for the victim.

In addition, the family served as a unit of economic co-operation. For instance, the head or other senior members of the family co-operated in working the family ponds and farmlands. During periods of poor harvest more fortunate family members contributed foodstuff to the affected members.

Although then the family was basically a socio-economic unit, it also had political aspects. Thus minor disputes or misu nderstanding within the family were often settled by the family head or by any designated elder in the absence of the family head.

Disputes between members of two families were also negotiated or mediated by the family heads, and only if they could not be resolved at this level were they taken to the House. These political functions of the family head made the family the testing ground for a man's potential in the community at large[1].

---

1. Informants were:
   i. Mr. Sokari Adewari, circa 65 years, @ Idema, 25/2/92;
   ii. Mr. Alfred Samuel, circa 72 years, @ Obeduma, 4/4/85

4.2 The House (Oghol-Otu)

The "House" (Oghol-otu), was a group made up of several families whose heads trace descent from a common founding ancestor through the female line.

At the head of every House was a House Head (Okei-Otu), who was selected by members of that House on the basis of ripe age and wisdom. When chosen he was presented to the King (Olilaema) in the village meeting house (igula) for an investiture ceremony which of course included the administration of an Oath of Allegiance to both the living and the dead by the Kin g himself or whoever he chose to do that amongst his cabinet chiefs on his behalf.

Once installed, the House Head could then perform the roles ascribed to his office. The House Head performed economic roles as well as political ones. He distributed or apportioned the House Land at every farming season and ensured the control of such land against encroachments and trespass from other houses.

The House was an important socio-political unit. Iduma burial laws allowed the burial expenses of a deceased to be borne by the family. Hence, the House Head co-ordinated members of his House in the burial of a deceased member whenever death occurred.

Disputes within the House were settled by the House Head and other senior members of the House. Also, the House Head interceded in matters between House members and non-members. For instance, minor cases, such as adultery were sometimes settled by the House Head, although in most instances, a neutral third party did[2].

4.3 The Village/Town (Ema)

The village/town (Ema) as the case may be was another important socio-political unit in this period. As we have earlier discussed, Iduma community consists of villages. These villages had their respective heads to

---

2. Informants were:

i. Chief John I. E. Adiboko, circa 81 years, Idema, 10/8/11
ii. Elder Lionel Joel Edumologbo, circa 78 years, Idema, 11/8/05

whom their subjects owe allegiance to. The Olilaema of Idema, is usually selected from amongst men who could trace their descent on the matrilineal line from the early King Igoniwari, while his deputy (Ipali-Olilaema) was chosen from the Ebo lineage.

The candidates for Olilaema and Ipali-Olilaema of Iduma, and any of the other communities were expected to be men of outstanding qualities. They were supposed to be honest, diligent and with no taint of witch craft. Anyone who did not come up to these standards would be rejected by the gods and the ancestors.

Once they had been selected and the necessary coronation ceremony performed they were hence forth addressed by the title Olilaema and Ipali-Olilaema respectively by all their subjects.

In the village assembly (igula), where the Olilaema of Idema sat with the House or lineage heads of his community he presided over all deliberations. The Olilaema was regarded as th e intermediary between the living members of the community and the ancestors and gods, and was believed to communicate between the two worlds. It was because of this that he was also expected to act as the high priest of the community.

In this capacity and in conjunction with his house heads, he decided on matters of rituals aimed at promoting communal welfare, and presided over the two annual festivals namely, eyal ilobhiri (eyal odudul) and eyal-awani, which fall in March and August respectively. The eyal-ilobhiri or eyal odudul as known amongst the Idumas of Abureni was a notable festival celebrated by most Abureni communities.

The system of village government was highly democratic, and involved not just the Olilaema and his Council of Chiefs (lineage heads) but the entire men and women of the villages. The women however, played a subordinate role. Thus they did not join their male counterparts in the deliberations in the village meeting house.

However, whenever any decision was taken in the Assembly and they found it unfavourable, they usually met elsewhere in the town and selected three to four representatives who spoke their minds to the entire Assembly. As a result the earlier decision might be reconsidered.

All laws, enactments and proclamations were made in the name of the town council which comprised of all the lineage groups or House Heads and the King (Olilaema). This council was a supreme body where aggrieved members of the public sought redress.

A wide variety of cases both criminal and civil was handled by the council. A case of murder once it was proved was punishable by compensating the victim's family with either a man or woman as a replacement for their murdered kinsman. An attempt to murder by threat of matchet and gun was also viewed seriously. In this case the penalty was a fine of twelve bottles of gin (igba-amin).

In a case of theft the accused was arraigned before the village/town Assembly as the case may be and publicly tried by the Council of House Heads and the entire Assembly. Finally, if the accused was found guilty he was fined and made to pay the equivalent of the value of the stolen property. If he was unable to pay, members of his family did. After this he was tied hands and feet and publicly flogged. It was so done because stealing was considered a disgrace not only to the thief but to his entire family. In addition, if he was a member of any social club, for instance, the Ekine Society, he was made to pay a fine of gin for hu miliating the association. He also received some punishments from his age group.

Finally, the thief and the stolen items, together with empty snail shells, tied around his waist and local chalk (amelem), robbed on his body. He was ordered to raise a song specially composed for the occasion and his age group made up the chorus. He was then paraded round the town with singing and clapping.

Cases of rape were also decided by the village/town Assembly. Cases of rape were not common but if any occurred was viewed with great seriousness.

The penalty was payment of fine to the girls (victim's) parents or the husband concerned if the girl was married. If the woman was fast asleep at the time sexual intercourse took place (ogionan), it is viewed as a form of rape since the consent of the women was not obtained.

In such circacumstance, which is common amongst married couples, certain rituals involving seven (7) young rats whose eyes had not been opened were used.

In addition to this ritual which the accused had to pay for, he was rubbed with local chalk on the face and paraded round the town with humiliating songs[3].

4.4 Town Wide Institution

Sekiapu (dancing people) or Ekine is one of such institutions in the town. This is a masking society which origin is linked to the legendary Kalabari woman Ekineba, who taught her town people to perform masquerades. The group's primary function consists of staging masquerades which climaxes with a festival that includes all the masks[4].

---

3. Elder Sokari Adewari, circa 65 years, personal interview at Idema,
   25/2/92
4. Martha G. Anderson: "Visual Arts" in The Land and people of Bayelsa
   State: Central Niger Delta, ed. E. J. Alagoa, (1999), pages 133 - 134

Tradition indicates that the Ekine Society's existence is quite old in Iduma, and those interviewed could not tell the exact period it was formed in Iduma. The rhetorical responses often gotten from individuals had been "to ascertain when Iduma started making or staging masquerades".

In addition to its primary functions the Ekine Society operated alongside the town Assembly in deciding certain cases brought before it.

Ekine Society was a socio-cultural organization whose membership was open to members of the public.

Interested members of the community join the society voluntarily upon payment of membership fees and fulfillment of other prescribed obligations.

Minor cases involving theft, assault, slander etc were tried by the society. Appeal could be made to the village/town Assembly, if any party felt dissatisfied with Ekine rulings.

Not all cases were handled by the village council and general assembly. There were cases that were settled by the family or by the House. It was only if these cases could not be settled by these bodies successfully that complainants/plaintiffs approached the Ekine Society. Cases that the Ekine Society could not settle were taken to the village Assembly.

However, there was no conscious effort to organize the community into age-groups for a variety of purposes. From time to time male and female members of the community were organized for general work for the benefit of the entire community. It was only during wrestling tournaments that division into age groups was observed, and opponents of the same age had to wrestle together.

4.5 Economy and Society

The economic set up of these early times helped to build and influence the socio-political set up of the town/village. The three principal political units, the family, House and the town, also served as units for economic co-operation, and the pattern of co-operation in turn helped to shape the characteristic of each of these units.

Although some land and some of the smaller forest ponds were owned by individuals, the bulk of both land and water resources were owned and allocated by families, Houses and the town. Thus much of the land and many of the ponds were owned and allocated by families and Houses, whilst the swamps (abarah), open rivers and creeks belonged to the town. The individual's dependence on these larger groups for access to vital means of livelihood reinforced their importance in his eyes.

Family, House, and Town were also important in providing the basic work groups.

The family was perhaps the most important unit of economic co-operation particularly, in the spheres of farming and palm oil production.
Marriage ties between families also provided an important basis for co-operation.

Having co-operated to produce foodstuff, members of the family came together to share them. In large families, more fortunate members also came to the aid of those who had suffered calamities such as loss of crops.

The House, too, was an important unit of economic co-operation. During the dry season, House fish-ponds were jointly baled by all members of the House that owned them and the fish so caught was distributed among the members. If a member of a particular House killed a big animal, it was his close kin and fellow House members that were first called upon to transport the game from the bush to town.

The carcass was not eaten by the hunter but shared with his House members. The sense of belonging to a group sharing strong economic interests gave rise to social co-operation between House members at times of marriage and burial ceremonies. The financial burden was faced collectively by the House members. These forms of economic co-operation enhanced the strength and solidarity of the House.

At the community level too, there was a high degree of economic co-operation which cut across the division between the Houses. Thus if it was a man's turn to process his palm oil he might call in a work-party drawn from all sections of the town. A similar community-wide work-party could also be called in to assist a man who was putting up a building. These are just two of many instances in which the individual was able to get help in his economic enterprises on a community wide basis. Such help did much to make the town seem important to its members.

In Iduma, the basic means of making a living were readily available to all. This meant that there weren't many factors making for differentiation in levels of wealth. It also meant that economic dependence of the majority upon a minority could not easily develop.

These economic circacumstances worked against any concentration of political power in the hands of a majority at this time. And this perhaps is why Iduma did not undergo the political centralization seen in some of the neighbours such as Nembe and Kalabari.

CHAPTER 5
IDUMA IN THE PERIOD BEFORE COLONIAL RULE
(1800AD – 1899AD)

This chapter discusses the economic and the socio-political developments that arose out of the decline and the abolition of the Trans Atlantic Slave Trade, and the rise of the Palm Oil Trade; and also, the fierce competition that ensued between the coastal middlemen and the contending "imperial forces" represented by the Royal Niger Company. In all cases Iduma as produc ers never had a fair deal in the trade but served the interest of the coastal middlemen (local monopolists) in the first instance, and secondly that of a global trade system represented by the biggest monopolist, the Royal Niger Company.

5.1 Economic Changes

On the West African Coast, the 19th Century saw a slow but successful change over from slave trade to the trade in palm produce (palm oil and kernels). Since the fresh water area of the Niger was richly endowed with oil palm trees, it was well placed to play a prominent role in the new trade.

During the period Iduma like several other Abureni and Ogbia communities became involved in this trade. Palm oil and kernels from Iduma were carried to the coastal ports of Brass and Akassa, where they were sold to European merchants. Oral tradition is very clear as to the role of Iduma as major producers of palm oil and kernel for this trade.

In the early years of Iduma's involvement in the trade, the okemegha system of production was employed to meet the initial demands. As we saw earlier, the system of production basically involved the drying of the palm fruits and their subsequent fermentation and pounding after which water was used to se parate the fibre and kernels from the oily substance, and the oilly substance was finally cooked to produce the oil.

Before long the increasing demand for palm produce by the Europeans on the coast, coupled with a growing awareness of the time wasting and tedious nature of the okemegha, gave way to a new faster system of production. In the event, the method devised of the old okunu system was hitherto, used for the production of oil on a small scale. This modified okunu system relied on certain newly introduced European manufactured materials, namely, tripod pot, (okpoin), bowls (abafu), drum (adrum), knife (ogie).

The modified okunu system involved working on large quantity of Palm fruits whilst they were still fresh. The palm fruits were separated from their stalks and cooked in tripod pots (okpoin), and drum. They were then turned into an unwidened canoe (okporogum), and pounded with legs, whilst water was added.

Once the fruits had been properly pounded, they were turned into a big canoe at the water side, and river water added, enabling easy skimming of the resultant oily fluid (ibobo-amunu). The latter was collected and cooked again with some vegetables to produce sweet-scented edible oil.

This new method was less energy-sapping than either the okemegha system or the old okunu system. It was also more efficient in terms of the quantity that could be produced per head of labour in any given time. In this way, Iduma producers were able to meet the increased demand from the coastal ports of Brass and Akassa.

Although Iduma people were heavily involved in production for the new trade, they played little or no part in transporting the product to the coast and selling it to the Europeans.

These roles were monopolized by Nembe men who acted as middlemen due to their long established commercial relationship with the Europeans. It has often been said that the coastal middlemen were completely opposed to European entry into the hinterland. And this does seem to have been true of the Nembe chiefs. Usually then, Iduma producers sold their oil to Nembe middlemen who came to the community to buy. It was only when their Nembe customers failed to turn up and they felt desperate did the Iduma producers take their oil out of the community for sale. And even then, they went no nearer the coast than Nembe.

Nembe traders gave Iduma producers such articles as beads, knives, hats, salt, basins, cotton, clothes, jugs, rum, gin, and sometimes guns and gun-powder in exchange for their oil. The trade was mainly barter. But currencies such as the manila (okp okiduma), the cowry (okoba), and J. J. W. Peters gin were used to some extent as mediums of exchange.

Notwithstanding the difficulties involved in the method of exchange people still showed enthusiasm in producing more oil to the coast because of the cosmetic attraction of the new trade.

Individuals who were extremely industrious actually accumulated a considerable share of the aforementioned European goods. The possession of domestic utensils such as jugs, basins, pots, and even clothing, hats and walking sticks were regarded as a mark of wealth and success. These attractions and the urge to make profits out of the produce, consequently led more people to abandon their previous occupations to the new trade.

From about 1876, the Brass River trade in palm oil had begun to feel the impact of European penetration of the hinterland markets. The situation became even worse after 1886, when the British government granted the Royal Niger Company (RNC) a charter giving it monopoly trading rights in large areas of the Delta and hinterland.

In the 1890's one of the bitterest complaints of Nembe traders against the Royal Niger Company was that it prevented them from trading with their immediate Ijaw, Abureni, and Ogb ia neighbours who produced cocoyams, plantain, and palm produce[1].

It was these frustrations that finally led Nembe to organize the 1895 raid on the Company's headquarters at Akassa. The strategy of the Nembe people was to take the

---

1. E. J. Alagoa, The Small Brave City State, (1964), page 60

war into the enemy's door step, which may have been well thought out to achieve certain strategic objectives.

Although the raid achieved its immediate goal of destroying the company's headquarters and eliminating the personnel, it was followed by devasting British reprisals against the Nembe community. As a result, most of the Nembe chiefs who had taken part were forced to flee their town.

As reported, both sides may have incurred loses but it was more devasting for the Nembes who had their town burnt, three of their war canoes sunk, thirty canons blown up, numbers of their people killed and wounded, and trade stopped[2].

With most of the Nembe middle men in hiding, there was a considerable decline in commercial activities at the Brass and Akassa Ports. This compelled Iduma producers to turn to suc h other growing centres as Abonnema. This new direction is said to have produced

---

2. J. U. J. Asiegbu, Nigeria and its British invaders, 1851 – 1920, Enugu, (1984) page 123

some significant changes in the prices of the palm produce. The middlemen were gradually eliminated and the people dealt directly with the various European firms[3].

The trade in palm produce was characterized by monopoly. At one end by the Niger Company when it was granted a charter by the British Government. This has been emphasized by many, including this writer; for instance, Professor Asiegbu dealt with the issue in his book in an extract dealing with a private letter written by Sir Claude M. Macdonald to Mr. Hill lamenting the frustrations of the native producers against the monopolists especially – the Royal Niger Company which he described as the biggest monopolist of the crowd[4].

---

3. Collins Daniel, An Economic and Political History of Idema.

From Early Times to present, unpublished thesis for the award of

B. A. degree in History, Uniport, (1985), page 49

4.   J. U. J. Asiegbu, (supra) page 122 – 125

EXTRACT: No. 1.

THE BRITISH ATTACK ON BRASS AS SEEN FROM A PRIVATE LETTER: MACDONALD'S RESENTMENTS ABOUT THE ROYAL NIGER COMPANY AND ITS MACHINATIONS.

My dear Hill,

Your letter of the 22nd (to hand yesterday) was most cheering. The atmosphere and surroundings generally have not been cheerful lately. The death of two of my poor chaps, both young fellows in the prime of life, was a great blow to me; they were only ill a couple of days, and the end in both cases was very sudden, one died on a Friday and the other the following Sunday, and my dispatches to the Foreign Office were written with an accompaniment of hammering the reverse of cheerful. However, it's all in the day's march and "que sera sera".

With regard to this Brass palaver it will be ancient history, and will have assumed a new phase long before this reaches you.

The Brassmen have undoubtedly had the fear of the Lord instilled into them, principally by means of the shell fire, also the 21-pr. rockets. I was told by an Okrika man who happened to be in Nembe the day before the attack when we were getting their range from Sacrifice Island, and two of the Niger Coast Protectorate 7-pr. shells fell in the town and burst. He said, "Plenty people fall for ground, plenty people be drunk become sober one time". My informant got into his canoe and cleared hastily.

On the occasion of the attack on Sacrifice Island one 3-pr. shell burst in a canoe, killing five and mortally wounding four; these canoes hold from forty to sixty men, all pretty well huddled up, which will account for the destruction caused by so small a projectile.

The Brass people cannot make out why their town was burnt and the other half only shelled and then left. I am bound to say the same surprised me very much. All arrangements had been made, and reinforcements of men, ammunition, and commissariat were coming up in streams, when one Gamble, R. N., came to the latter and said that he thought that enough valuable lives had been lost, and that we should retire; at the time we had taken and burnt half of the town; but the other half (called Bassambiri) was blazing away merrily with cannon and rifle fire from the other side of a creek on which it is situated, getting horrib ly pounded in so doing by our 3-pr. quick–firing guns. I happened to overhear this near Gamble but said nothing, not thinking for a moment that the Admiral would listen to him, for only an hour before we had made arrangements for polishing of Bassa mbiri in the afternoon, and had settled upon a house in the Mission in closure in which to pass the night. I even got my cook up with his pots and pans, and started him at cooking the evening meal.

The Admiral came to me and said that he had thought it out, and was of the opinion that we had now better retire; naturally I was a bit surprised, and suggested that as we had got to the place it would be as well to stop there, say, twenty-four hours, and, indeed, under instructions from him, had made all arrangements so to do; then Gamble, R. N., came up and said that he thought sufficient valuable lives had been lost; to this I replied that you could not make omelettes without breaking eggs, and that it was a very dangerous theory to start; that you could sail gaily into this sort of job and nobody get hurt, because when anybody did get knocked over you were very apt to think that the other side were not playing the game, and go off in a huff; this theory was then withdrawn.

The Admiral then said to me that his instructions were to punish the Brassmen for the outrage committed, and that he c onsidered that the wish to keep his men in that fever swamp another evening.

As my instructions were to act in concert with the Admiralty, I had no answer to make to the above. In his heart of hearts the Admiral, who is full of go and pluck, was for going on, but I think, having lost three men, he feared the Admiral, and did not like the chance of losing anymore. With regard to his argument that the Brassmen had been sufficiently punished for the outrage they had committed, I am bound to say I am heartily in accord with him. Their Twon Nembe, which they looked upon as impregnable, as did all the Niger tribes, was taken in a few hours (it would have been a matter of weeks had we given them a few more days to get ready). The town was burnt; three of their war canoes sunk; thirty cannon blown up; numbers of their people killed and wounded; two of their stockade towns blown to smithsereens; and all the Chiefs' houses in a third blown up with gun-cotton. Their entire trade has been stopped (and is still stopped) since the 29th January; they have given up twenty-one cannons and fifteen more cannons; twenty-five prisoners, which I thought had been eaten, as well as nine boats, the machine guns, & c., which they looted from the Niger Company. But I think the withdrawal from Nembe when the whole thing lay at our feet was a pity, for the African mind cannot grasp the argument of "as you are strong be merciful". I have squared this argument by taking the sudden withdrawal upon myself, and telling them, (the Chiefs) that at the last moment I begged for them, and that at my earnest request the Admiral stayed his hand. This, I believe, they have tumbled to. But, in the meanwhile, the Niger Company's people (local) say that we were practically beaten out of Nembe, and that I advised the retreat. Fortunately I am accustomed to the African liar, and know his immense capabilities.

By the last mail I got a cutting from The Times, headed " The Rising in the Niger Protectorate", very cleverly compiled, but somewhat untrue, as the following facts put side by side with the text will show. "The rising of the natives at Brass, in the Niger Protectorate, and their organized raid across the frontier into the peaceful Territory of the Niger, render necessary" & c. there had been severe fighting on the banks of the Niger about a week before the organized raid – the Niger Company can supply exact date – in which an English officer in the service of the Royal Niger Company had been severely wounded, and eight men of the constabulary killed or wounded. This officer, Captain Morgan, I saw and spoke to at Akassa. The fight took place between the Company's troops and an Ejoh village. This is one of numerous scrimmages which are constantly taking place in the Nige r, but which are never reported, all officials of the Company being bound down to secrecy – in their contracts a most useful proviso. About three months ago another fight took place up the Niger, in which the Royal Niger Company had sixteen men killed. Some little time, about a year ago, they had a fight near our Warri boundary, and brought their wounded (eight) to the Vice-Consulate; said wounded were treated by Dr. Roth, the Protectorate surgeon. One man was mortally wounded, and died, and is buried in the Protectorate cemetery at Brass.

Jaja was deported (and very rightly) by H.H. Johnson because he was a big monopolist, and threatened to become bigger. Nana was knocked endways by Moor and the gun-boats for the very same reason, and now we have wiped the floor with the Brassmen because they have endeavoured to go for the biggest monopolist of the crowd – the Royal Niger Company. As I daresay you are aware, in the vast territories of the Niger Company there is not one single outside trade, black, white, green or yellow. The markets are all theirs. They can open or shut any given market at will, which means subsistence or starvation to the native inhabitants of the place. They can offer any price they like to the producers, and the latter must either take it or starve. And why, in heaven's name, why? Because they (the Company) must pay their 6 or 7 percent to the shareholder. Why shouldn't th e wretched producer sell his stuff to the best advantage, and to whom he likes? He is the aboriginal of the country, and the tree on which the palm-nut grows is his. No. He must sell it to the C ompany or starve. Then throughout the territories there are tho usands of native villages all engaged in the palm oil trade, or w ould like to be, for the oil is growing at their doors; but the port s of entry, at which only they are allowed to trade, are in compa rison very few in number, so that there are tracts of oil-produci ng country not worked at all. Why not pay your duty at the doo r and trade where you like? This is the case at Accra, Lagos, the Protectorate, Cameroons, & c ....

However, my dear old chap, I won't go on any more on the papers; George Goldie can. Personally I have nothing to say against the Niger Company, but I think all these companies are most unfair on the natives, the principal of them I mean.

The Brassmen are wild cannibals when their blood is up, but that they have been damned badly treated from start to finish there is no possible doubt whatever, and I am prepared t o prove it up to the hill. The Brassmen are quite prepared to pa y their duty and trade alongside whitemen, but they are not all owed.

Yours ever,

(Signed): Claude M. Macdonald

5.2 The Impact of the Akassa War

The Akassa War prosecuted by the Brass (Nembe) people led by their ruler, King Frederick William Koko, Mingi VIII, against the British, resulting on the attack of the Royal Niger Company depot at Akassa on 29th January, 1895 was premised on some grievances. The attack which expectedly, resulted to a counter attack on Nembe in February, 1895 undoubledly produced some consequences not limited to the direct parties in the war but to its (Nembe) immediate neighbours on the North East – the Iduma people.

However, before I begin to deal with the specific impact of the war on Iduma it will be necessary to state some of the causes of the war which the colonial authorities referred to as the " Akassa Raid". It is my view that what happened could not have been described as "a raid except for the usual intention of Europeans to always lampoon or paint Africans black in matters of t his nature with a view to make the public see the Africans as the aggressor. The whole intention of such writers was aimed at indicting King Frederick William Koko and his men. In military parlance, once there was an attack by one party which had resulted to a counter attack by the other, the situation can no longer be described otherwise but as war. This seems to be the situation of the Akassa War of 1895. I therefore submit that the proper name of the conflict is the "Akassa War", and it ought to be called the Akassa war rather than Akassa raid.

The memorandum presented by the people of Nembe to an official inquiry conducted on 8th June 1895 by Sir John Kirk seems to have captured their principal grievances. Part of their memorandum herein reproduced, read thus:

"A few months after this he (Consul Hewett) came back again and to our great surprise informed us that the government had granted to the National African Company, a royal charter on the River Niger which meant that they had full power to do what they liked in the River, and to impose and receive duties from everybody who wished to go there for the purpose of trade. We called his attention to the fact of our Treaty (in March 1886) which states that trade was free, how was it then that we were not allowed to go and trade freely at villages the people of who m our Fathers, Grandfathers and we had traded within past times......

We have suffered many hardships from the company's reputation, our people have been fired upon by the Niger Company's launches, they have been fired upon from the Niger Company's hulks, our canoes have been seized and goods taken, sometimes when engaged in what the white man called smuggling and sometimes when not..........

Traders we are, have been, and always will be. The soil of our country is too poor to cultivate sufficient food for all our people, and so if we do not trade and get food from other tribes we shall suffer great want and misery"[5].

Whilst not trying to justify the Brass (Nembe) people for their violent action of 29th January 1895, but considered against the circacumstance they found themselves, it was compulsive that they needed to do something to register their grave grievances against the excesses of the RNC, since all diplomatic approaches seemed to have failed.

---

5. See J. U. J. Asiegbu, op. cit. pages 102 – 104

The option open to them was to take their destinies in their hands. Hence, they decided that instead of waiting for hunger to exterminate them, they preferred dying on the battle field.

Accordingly, on 29th January 1895, King Frederick William Koko, Mingi VIII, reportedly, mobilized an armada of thirty-one (31) war canoes and attacked the Royal Niger Company depot at Akassa[6]. This was swiftly followed by a counter-attack by the British on February 1895.

The special Commissioner, Sir John Kirk appointed by the United Kingdom Government to investigate matters relating to the "Akassa War" in June 1895, came to the conclusion that King Koko and his people had a legitimate grievance. Kirk, however, blamed the British Government whose charter the Royal Niger Company used to oppress people within its jurisdiction[7].

---

7. Tekena N. Tamuno, Oil Wars in the Niger Delta (1849 – 2009), Ibadan, 2011, page 52, Akassa war

Having stated the grievances that led to the war, what then was the impact of this war on Iduma. Very many writers had glossed over this aspect, but like every war the effect on nearby communities cannot be ruled out.

The impact of the war was therefore not limited to the two principal parties namely, Nembe, and the RNC aided by the British Government, but extended also to the Iduma people that share a north east boundary with Nembe.

There are strong indications pointing to the fact that some Iduma men participated in the Akassa War. There are traditions linking most of the dreaded charms and amulets deployed by the Nembe warriors for the war to Iduma medicine men. The abula charm that had the potency of making a warrior invisible before his enemies extensively used by the Nembe warriors had its route from Iduma, the source maintained[8].

---

8. Dakipre Garrick, circa 63 years, Oboghe, 5/2/15. Daniel Oruan, circa 101 years, @ Idema, 25/2/76 by personal interview

While not doubting the power of black magic, there were still causalities on the side of Nembe. The argument is that since Iduma also participated and suffered losses of men at the war, the impact could not have been limited to Nembe and the Royal Niger Company alone.

The war was said to have also caused apprehension in the Nembe country and beyond, and became a thing of worry an d concern to all. This of course, led to heightened tension coupled with the noise of heavy shelling of canons and bombardments in Nembe[9].

With most of the Nembe middle men especially the war canoe chiefs that participated in the attack in hiding, it led to considerable decline in commercial activities within Brass-Nembe trading area. This compelled the Iduma producers to turn to more distant centres such as Abonnema to sell their produce. As earlier mentioned, Abonnema then became the new focus for active business activities.

---

9. Ibid.

Perhaps the most outstanding impact which has continued to echo in various traditions both in Iduma and Nembe was the massive destruction in Nembe that led many to flee the community into taking refuge in Iduma farmlands/settlements such as Obhietia (Obiata), Emata-Oruan (Atubo), Asaga (Agada), Ogbomasaga (Sangapiri): Chief Keremah and his family took refuge in Obhietia (Obiata), an old settlement of Ebo of Idema, used by family members for farming, hunting and canoe carving. Chief Febo on the other hand ran to Oruan (Atubo 1), otherwise called Emata-Oguru and popularly known as Atubo settlement where he took refuge under members of the Egberi, and Okikia yun lineages of Idema who had established the settlement for farming and other economic activities. Similarly, Chief Christopher Iwowari also of Bassambiri approached his friend Chief Opuso of Obeduma and sought for refuge for members of his family and personal servants at Asaga (Agada), a settlement founded by Opuso[10].

I consider this impact as outstanding having regard to the issue of settlers and host communities, refugees and its wider implications. In most parts of the World up to present times, the incidence of war has always produced refugees, and the Akassa War was not an exception. The war indeed produced many refugees who were protected by the Iduma people in their territories.

At the end of the war, while some decided to return to Bassambiri Nembe, majority found these settlements more appealing for their economic activities, and decided to stay back.

5.3   Political Developments

The fact that Iduma participated in the Atlantic Palm Produce trade almost exclusively as producers and

10. HRH Simeon M. A. Opuso, personal interview, 12/08/1984

not as executors of produce to the coast meant that, although most able bodied men became a little wealthier, there were more of the great concentrations of wealth that developed at Nembe.

This was understandable because the coastal middlemen in the trade and the European trading firms were the ones that dictated the terms of trade, rather than the local producers. As a result, there was little in the way of new political civilization. The socio-political organization indeed, remained much as it had been before the era of Nembe economic dominance.

In an attempt to establish an imperial control of Iduma, the Nembe middlemen ensured that the trade was perpetually in their hands, and so it was until the trade declined due to the Akassa War. They (the Nembes) constantly sought to dominate the area by preventing Iduma people from having direct contact with the Europeans at the coast.

Similarly, in later years when the Royal Niger Company took over the monopoly of the palm oil and kernels trade from the coastal middlemen, majority of Iduma men, attracted to the trade still maintained the role of producers.

The vast territory of the Niger was monopolized by the Royal Niger Company. They controlled the markets. They opened and shut markets at will, which meant subsistence or starvation to the native inhabitants of the place. They offered any price they liked to the producers, and the latter must either take it or starve. The wretched producer was not allowed to sell his stuff to the best advantage, and to whom he likes, but either to sell to the company or starve.

I contend therefore that the trade was skewed towards making the coastal middlemen and lately, the Europeans wealthier rather than the Idumas who were largely local producers. It was a trade of unequal exchange which served specific interests, that of the costal middlemen and that of a global trade system which centres were in Europe and America. This development is consistant with Walter Rodney's argument when he said " Trade with Africa actually helped Europe to weld together more closely the different national economies, but in Africa there was disruption and disintegration at the local level. At the same time, its local economy ceased to be directed exclusively or even primarily towards the satisfaction of the wants of its inhabitants … their economic effort served external interest and made them dependent on those external forces based in Western Europe. In this way, the African economy taken as a whole was diverte d away from its previous line of development and became distorted"[11].

5.4 Economy and Society

Despite the demands of the Trans Atlantic palm oil trade, Iduma continued with her traditional occupations. However, these demands did not encourage many to become full-time producers of oil.

---

11. Walter Rodney, How Europe Under-developed Africa, Washington, DC.
Howard University Press, (1974), page 109

In the circumstances, less attention was given to the other occupations. Thus, the surpluses recorded in such other occupations gradually reduced since most households spent more of their time in the oil industry. In spite of this reduction, households were still able to sustain themselves from the little they produced and depended also on their neighbours for those commodities they lacked.

On a general level, the economic transition to large-scale palm oil production did make a few individuals wealthier.

The few individuals who were opportuned to have made profits were able to use that in erecting somewhat fine buildings with corrugated iron sheets, as well as contracting big dowry marriages within and outside their immediate localities. Oral tradition also talks of certain people who acquired servants from the Igbo country with their wealth.

The usual question asked is that can these gains be compared to that of the middlemen and what the European monopolists gained out of the trade? The answer to this is most likely, to be in the negative and I hold the same view.

Again, the so called new concentrations of wealth do not also appear to have been sufficient to bring about the emergence of a new political class or leadership, and the establishment of new political offices as it happened in some other societies.

The individual, "family" and "House" still performed their traditional functions. The family still very much acted as economic unit and the "House" and village still performed their traditional functions of assisting fellow villagers, who in turn reciprocated.

CHAPTER 6

IDUMA FROM THE BEGINNING OF COLONIAL RULE TO NIGERIA INDEPENDENCE (1900AD – 1960AD)

In the previous chapter I examined the economic and socio-political developments that arose out of the decline of the Atlantic slave trade and rise of the trade in Palm oil. I have argued that in both cases. Iduma served the interest of Nembe and Kalabari (New Calabar) middlemen who monopolized the trade and ultimately that of a global trade system with its centres in Europe and America.

In this chapter, I will examine the political, economic and social changes from the beginning of colonial rule to independence and the impact of all these on Iduma.

6.1 Political Developments

Here, as in other parts of what was to become Nigeria, the formal establishment of British administration took place piecemeal. In 1881 George Goldie had asked for a charter for his newly formed National African Company. It was refused. By 1886, however the situation had changed and his company was chartered as the Royal Niger Company, and it was Goldie who shaped the future colony of Nigeria[1]. The surrounding areas of the Delta were taken over and placed under British rule by the creation of the Oil Rivers Protectorate in 1887.

In 1893 these areas were renamed the Niger Coast Protectorate. From this time on, various punitive expeditions and treaties aimed at consolidating British rule were executed. Apart from the 1895 expedition against Nembe, following their raid on the Royal Niger Company depot at Akassa, King Ibanichuka, Ado VI, of Okrika was seized in 1896.

---

1. D. I. Rooney and E. Halladay, The building of Modern Africa, London:
George G. Harrap and Co. Ltd, (1967), page 47

In 1897 the ancient Benin Kingdom was over-run. Benin was independent until in 1897 when the British expedition entered the town[2].

In 1898 Chief Wogu of Umukoroshe was punished for closing the roads to interior markets against those who failed to pay him tolls[3]. Also, in 1897 Sir George T. Goldie personally led a successful expedition against Nupe and Ilorin and reduced them to submission.

By 1891 various vice-consuls had been stationed in places like Brass, Degema, Bonny, Calabar, etc. In December, 1899, the charter of the Royal Niger Company was revoked by the British Government.

---

2. Henry Willink et al, Report of the Commission appointed to enquire into the fears of Minorities and the means of allaying them, Her majority's stationery office, London, 1958, page 9
3. Wainbite E. Wariboko, "Social and Political Development", in Land and People of Nigeria: Rivers State, eds., E. J. Alagoa and T. N. Tamuno, Port Harcourt, (1989), page 128

Royal Niger Company territories which lay south of Idah, and in the same year the protectorate of Southern Nigeria was declared. By 1st January, 1900, the protectorate of Northern Nigeria was also formally declared, which led to the assumption of direct control over the area, thus giving way to the official declaration of colonial rule in Nigeria.

The 20th century was a fateful period in which British administrative ingenuity wrought changes either directly or indirectly. As soon as the protectorates of Nigeria were declared, the colonial government started introducing local government institutions in the different consular areas.

In the new administrative set up, the Iduma people were placed under the Brass consular authority being the Brass Division of the Owerri Province. The first attempt made to bring the government nearer the people began with the establishment of Native Courts from the existing Native Councils.

In the Brass Division, two Native Authorities covering the three district units namely: Native Authority (NA) for Twon, which was initially incorporated with the Brass Native Court area; the Nembe Native Court and Authority which covered, all the adjoining villages in Nembe; and Ogbia and the Ekowe native authority area[4].

This was the period when there was a quest by the British authorities for strong and powerful chiefs through whom to rule. Consequently, Chief Joseph Alagoa, became a ready tool in the hands of the colonial authorities. The said Chief was appointed Native Authority (NA) for Nembe Court area which compri sed not only Nembe but also Abureni, Odual and Ogbia who were non-Nembe groups.

The need for administrative convenience has also been alluded to as the reason behind the placing of small groups lacking strong chiefs under the nearest strong chiefs[5]. By this arrangement the colonial government

---

4. E. J. Alagoa, The Small Brave City State, (1964), page 119
5. Ukelonu O, Report of the Commission of Inquiry into the Nembe

Chieftaincy Dispute, Eungu, Eastern Region of Nigeria official

document No. 24, (1960), page 9

merged different groups irrespective of their cultures into single administrative units. This is how Iduma, having escaped Nembe and Kalabari political domination in the 19th century, came under Nembe domination in colonial times.

Protests however, in the second decade of the 20th century resulting from the discriminatory attitudes of the Nembe against the non-Nembe came to the ears of the colonial administration.

Apart from the discriminatory attitudes of Nembe against the non-Nembe, there were also cases of oppression and ill tr eatment against the non-Nembe people. For instance, within the period, some Kalabari Chiefs led by Chiefs Dick Harry Braide, Quaker Bob Manual and Ors representing the people of Saka, Kugbo, and Idema instituted a suit against Chiefs Egbelu and Allagoa of Brass representing the Chiefs of Brass and sought for a declaration that the people of Saka (Odual), Kugbo, and Idema and their property were under their control and authority. In the said matter they sought for injunction to restrain the Defendants being the Nembe people, their successors and representatives from exercising acts of authority over the said people or over their property.

The Defendants had claimed in the said matter that they owned the Idemas and their property, and the Idemas were their subjects.

When the matter was brought before the Supreme Court of the colony of the Protectorate of Southern Nigeria (Divisional Court) Calabar for adjudication, the pursne judge, His Honour Mr. Justice A.F.C. Webber, made the following observation: "It is quite possible that the IDEMAS may have regarded someone either at NEMBE or at NEW CALABAR as their master in the sense that they would be protected by him in case of external attack and in return for this have rendered service or paid tribute to one or other; but up to the time of the advent of the Governme nt, the IDEMAS had their kings who reigned in succession and represented the supreme head of the IDEMA people.... The crown had arrived to afford protection and to open trade to all. No one state was under the power and authority of any other state and it was not then necessary anymore to seek protection or assistance from anyone but from the crown[6].

The Court in the course of hearing the matter made the following findings:

1. The IDEMAS, KUGBOS and SAKAS and their property are not under the control or authority of the plaintiffs nor do they belong to the plaintiffs in the sense that they are members of plaintiff's houses.
2. The IDEMAS, KUGBOS and SAKAS were independent people and are still independent. There may have been alliances formed between the KUGBOS and SAKAS on the one hand and

---

6. See Chiefs Dick Harry Braide and Others Vs Chiefs Egbelu &

Allagoa of Brass, judgement delivered by the Supreme Court of the

Colony of the protectorate of Southern Nigeria, Calabar division, 3rd

March, 1913, page 5

3. That whatever tribute was paid or whatever services were rendered, this tribute and services were in return for protection they may have received and ceased at the advent of the British Government [7].

Following these findings the Supreme Court refused the declaration and injunction sought by the plaintiffs but rather granted costs to the Defendants which it fixed at 100 guineas.

In 1913 in a bid to forestall unrest in the area arising from the discriminatory attitudes of the Nembe against the non-Nembe an administrative committee was set up to study the political organization of the non-Nembe area which included Ogbia, Odual and Abureni with a view to establishing a separate court for them.

In 1915, a separate court was approved for Ogbia, and a similar one for Odual in 1921, but the Aburenis

---

7. See Chiefs Dick Harry Braide and Others Vs Chiefs Egbelu &

Allagoa, (Supra) were still retained in the Nembe Court area pending further inquiries into the history and the organization of their group[8].

Despite the several protests by the Abureni group of unfair treatment in the Nembe Court area the government was still adamant; hence in the 1930s, the Abureni group sent a delegation to Enugu to demand a separate Court. Although the efforts of the group were recognized and a Native Court approved for the Abureni area to be sited at Idema in 1932, internal intrigues over the matter led to the non realization of the proposed Native Court.

Having failed to sink their differences, the Abureni communities had no alternative but to continue attending the Nembe Native Court. Membership of the Nembe Native Court was dominated by the Nembe chiefs. Oral tradition is very emphatic on this aspect and maintains

---

8. E. N. Dickenson, Report on the Historical and Administrative Structure of Nembe, 1932, pages 24 – 25

that for the greater part of the Court's existence, the presidency of the Court was monopolized by the Nembe Chiefs. Although in principle the office of the president was rotational, in practice this was not the case since Nembe chauvinism dominated the electoral processes. Again, whilst all Nembe House heads were eligible for membership of the Native Court, only the heads of Houses of the non-Nembe communities were not eligible.

A slight improvement in the situation took place in the late 1930s, when a broader representation of the non-Nembe communities was introduced. A wide range of cases were decided in this court. First of all, it dealt with most cases involving native law and custom. In addition, it enforced statutory law and had a wide range of power in some criminal cases. Cases of murder, theft and slander previously decided by the kings and House heads were now a prerogative of the customary Court.

In the 1940s certain reforms were introduced all over the eastern provinces. Their aim being to bring the system of local government more in line with the non-centralized system of traditional government, so called in the area, and to reconcile the need for centralization with the multiplicity of traditional political units. During this period, in addition to the customary courts, local councils and district councils were created. These new councils unlike the previous ones had an elected membership.

In the 1950s, there were slight reforms. By 1953 the Native Administration Ordinance was repealed to establish the local government administration in the Eastern Region. By 1954 this new local government administration started functioning. Its provisions allowed for quicker political process whereby the people in the rural areas would also be involved in the administration.

By this provision, village councils were established in Iduma and in the other villages in Brass. Members were drawn from Idema, Eboh and Obeduma, to constitute the Iduma Council, while other persons were elected to represent each village at the district level. Notable names such as Messrs. Ogirirki Ogoli, Ekitei Wellington Ogbomade, Daniel Offor, Robert Offor and Reuben Edoghotu, were said to have represented Iduma at different times as councillors.

Between 1954 and 1957, direct elections based on universal adult suffrage were introduced in the Eastern Region, and candidates for elective posts, thenceforth contested for seats on political party platforms[9]. During this period, three dominant political organizations, patterned on ethnic and Regional formations, were in control of each of three regions. The National Council for Nigeria and the Cameroons (NCNC) was the dominant party in the East under the able leadership of Dr. Nnamdi Azikiwe. The Action Group (AG) under the leadership of Chief Obafemi Awolowo was firmly in control of the Yoruba dominated Western Region. While in the North the Northern Peoples Congress (

NPC) led by the Sardauna of Sokoto controlled the Hausa-Fulani dominated Northern Region.

---

9. R. L. Sklar, Nigerian Political Parties, 1983, pages 28 – 31
    In the defunct Eastern Region, the election that was conducted between 1953 and 1957 at both the regional and the federal levels was dominated by the National Council for Nigeria and the Cameroons (NCNC).

At the elections of 1953 the NCNC won 72 out of 84 seats, the rest going to four different opposition groups. In 1954 there were elections to the House of Representatives; of the 42 seats, the NCNC won 30, UNIP 3, the Action Group (AG) 4 and Independents 5. In March, 1957, there were elections to the Eastern House of Assembly at which the NCNC won 63 seats out of 84, the Action Group 15,
UNIP 5, and there was one Independent[10].

By 1958, a new political organization the Niger Delta Congress (NDC) was formed from the Cross Rivers, Ogoja and Rivers (COR) State Movement, but was spear-headed by Rivers State Movement elements. The NDC in preparation for the 1959 Federal elections had to fill in candidates in the various constituencies.

10. Henry Willinks, op cit, page 36

In the Brass area, Iduma was not fortunate to have produced any candidates, but other neighbouring villages did. Especially in the Ogbia District where Chief Melford Obiene Okilo emerged to contest the Brass Federal Constituency on the platform of the newly formed NDC.

The NDC in its campaigns promised self determination and freedom for the riverine people including Iduma. The party symbol or emblem was the fish, giving an indication that the party was pro-rivers people of which Iduma was a part of. Its campaign slogan was the creation of a separate Rivers State from the then Eastern Region if the riverine people were to free themselves from Ibo domination in all spheres of life[11].

The Action Group (AG) in particular promised free primary education and the establishment of a post-primary institution for Iduma to serve all the Abureni communities if voted into power. The NCNC whose base

---

11. Elijah Obinah, circa 68 years, personal interview, @ Obeduma, 5/9/90.

had already been taken over by the popular NDC promised to establish a dispensary and to provide employment opportunities for those who would want to make a career in the public service.

When at last the elections were held all over the federation in 1959, Iduma followed others to vote. Instead of the previous pattern of voting whereby the NCNC intimidated people to vote for it, it suffered a major setback since Iduma became more interested in Melford Obiene Okilo's candidacy and victory. Hence they voted massively for the NDC candidate who fortunately, swept the polls for the Brass Federal Constituency. At the federal level, the NPC was victorious, but in order to form a broad based National government, the Sir Alhaji Tafawa Balewa NPC allied with the NCNC. In order to assure the colonial authorities that the minorities were part of the National Government, the NPC also forged an alliance with the NDC, which won a single seat in that election [12].

---

12. Melford O. Okilo, Personal interview, Port Harcourt, 20/06/2003

The stage having been set for independence, in early 1960, a Constitutional Conference was held in London which prece eded Nigeria's formal political independence on 1st October, 1960.

Although the politicians who made their promises during the electioneering campaigns were never seen again in Iduma, the news of Nigeria's independence was greeted with great jubilations.

Having little voice at local government level and none at all at either regional or the federal levels, and seeing no benefits from any of these levels, Iduma turned their attention once more to their own traditional institutions of town government.

6.2 Economic Changes

Needless to re-emphasize that the real reason behind the British colonization crusade of Africa was more for economic reasons than the much taunted "civilizing mission". It is the view of some African scholars that the "Niger territory or area" which Flora Shaw (later Lady Lugard) had used in her London Times Publication of 8th January, 1897, calling on the British Government to colonize the territory rested on considerations which were more economic than political[13].

The economic changes brought about by British action during the colonial period, forms the thrust of our discussion in this segment.

The beginning of the colonial era did not stop Iduma people from continuing to pursue their previous economic engagements, although from time to time new attractions were opened to them. In fact, the people continued with most of their previous economic activities, such as farming, fishing, canoe production, weaving of mats, baskets, thatches and most importantly, the production of palm oil and kernels.

---

13. N. C. Ejituwu and John H. Enemugwem, "Nigeria and the marginalization of the Niger Delta" in History Concourse 2007, the future of the Niger Delta. The search for a relevant Narrative, eds,. Abi Alabo Derefaka and Atei Okorobia, Port Harcourt, (2008), page 76.

Oral tradition however, indicates that although many people continued with the production of palm oil and kernels, some others took advantage of the decline of the Nembe middlemen and began to enter the palm produce trade[14]. With the decline of Nembe and Brass as buying centres and the rise of Abonne ma in their stead, the few Iduma traders were increasingly attracted to Abonnema.

The Nembe traders became very uncomfortable with these developments, and confronted the Iduma people with all sorts of threats[15]. Those who could not bear the arduous task of travelling the long distance to Abonnema (a day pulling as against 4 hours to Nembe) continued to sell their produce at Nembe. Nonetheless, the more energetic and adventurous traders ignored Nembe threats and went more and more to Abonnema.

At Abonnema the price of a casket of oil fluctuated

---

14. Tombibi Ikuli–Ene, circa 60 years, personal interview, @ Idema, 4/4/85
15. Ibid

from £1 in bad times to £20 in good times. The price of a tank of kernels fluctuated similarly. Nonetheless, prices were better than they were at Nembe and Brass. There was also a cheaper and more abundant supply of manufactured goods such as salt, clothes, soap, biscuits, etc. These were bought with some of the proceeds of the sale of produce, and either kept or resold at home.

In the late 1940s, the growing European demand for timber such as Iroko, Mahogany, Abura, Obeche etc, attracted many Iduma men into this timber extractive industry. Timber exploi tation in this area started at a time when the country had already been integrated into the monetary economy. Hence, in Iduma as elsewhere, labour recruitment for timber production was not done on the basis of reciprocal aid. Especially with the introduction of taxation, young men preferred to sell their labour for physical cash with which they could pay their taxes. Again, in their traditional occupations such as farming and palm oil and kernels production, they still continued to recruit labour on the old reciprocal basis. This was so because these economic activities entailed distributing the resultant crops or the palm oil to those who had participated in the production as members' work-groups and kin-groups in the process of production, and it was only the surplus that was sold. The case of timber, however, was different, since the entire product was sold and the money realized was not meant to be shared so freely with neighbours.

In this new venture, individuals who had accumulated sufficient capital from other economic activities used such capital to work the timber. Two to three or even four persons could pool their resources together for the purpose. They hired labourers who felled the trees in the forest, cut them into sizeable logs to various timber agents. According to one of my informants, who had himself been a timber producer, some people who did n ot have sufficient capital for hiring labour, got their initial capital on trust from Abonnema agents such as

one Mr. Dickson[16].

Another sector of the economy to undergo development during the period was the fishing industry.

In the early 20th Century, there was a remarkable change in fishing methods, when cast-nets, spread-nets, and dry-nets made of imported vegetable-fibre twine replaced the indigenous implements that had been used before. This change made for a new era of prosperity in fishing, since it promoted large catches of different types of fish such as saw-fish and sungu, which had been difficult to catch with earlier methods.

6.3 Social Changes

It has been argued that before the Berlin Conference however, as a direct result of the willingness and preparedness of Her Majesty's Consuls, Christian

---

16. Ebimawoto Daniel, circa 84 years, personal interview, @

Idema, 21/05/2014

Missionaries and European Merchants (the extra-territorial, trip artite forces of change) to intervene in the internal affairs of trad ing states in pursuit of their own imperial ideological interests i n the Niger Delta, the indigenous socio-political cultural and rel igious heritage, including the pre-existing world views and val ues that underpinned and nourished that heritage, came under severe interrogation[17].

The establishment of colonial rule in Nigeria brought ab out both positive and negative social changes in Iduma.

Culturally, European forms and patterns of behavior gai ned ground. In general, European ideas have made an enduring impact on the culture of Iduma people. The social structure, the thought system or world view and the mode of dress have bee n largely influenced by

---

17. Waibinte E. Wariboko, "The emasculation and transformation of indigenous governance and Leadership structure in the Eastern Niger Delta 1848 – 1960", in History Concourse 2007 the future of the Niger Delta: The search for relevant narrative eds. Abi Alabo, Derefaka and Atei M. Okorobia, Port Harcourt, (2009), page 96

European ideas. Colonialism greatly changed the society throug h the encouragement of Christianity and the formal

educational system. The spread of Christianity to Iduma was noticed in 1896 when the Anglican Church was formerly established by late Reverend J.D. Garrick. This feat was made possible through the effort of eleven (11) faithfuls led by Mr. Daniel Oruan. The others were, Graham Ake, David Isaiah, Ernest Robbin, Johnson Sokari, Koru Ibe, Akari Emagu, Frank Ibhughom, David Arugu, Brown Akari and George Okoni. They were attracted to the Christian religion while in Abonnema on a business trip. When the church was initially established, Mr. Daniel Oruan's residence was used for church services, including morning and evening prayer sessions[18].

Despite their initial persecution from the traditionalists, who objected to the establishment and growth of the church on grounds of their traditional

---

18. Source: Daniel Oruan family diary at Idema

religious beliefs and practices, membership of the church increased as more persons were attracted to its fold.

By 1910, a permanent church building had been built at Eme compound, in Idema. Also by 1927, a missionary school, St. John's (Anglican) School, had been established in Idema town as a result of the increase in the number of adherents to the new faith. However, the school suffered a great deal in the period as most parents hardly sent their children to the school since a majority of the people were against the church.

The Christian missions as we can see contributed much to social changes by the use of St. John's Anglican School, Idema, as a vehicle for change, since all those who passed through the school were exposed to European ideas and culture, and generally a civilized way of life.

The Christian missions not only helped the colonial government to check barbaric acts such as human sacrifice and the killing of twin babies but also helped to promote a stable and peaceful society. The gathering of people of different communities in the same school helped to overcome inter community prejudices which were very common, hitherto. For instance, it was not until the church gained momentum in Iduma that some of these practices were finally eliminated.

Another significant social change that the colonial administration brought about in Iduma was the reduction of inter-community feuds. Incidents of violent inter-community clashes were reduced during the colonial period. Iduma people learned to complain to the colonial authorities for redress instead of waging wars against their neighbours who offended them.

It is important to also observe that some social effects of colonialism were negative. One of such was the wholesale adop tion of European social and religious institutions. The colonial government while imposing alien institutions on the people, failed to appreciate the positive values of the people's culture. This neglect of the foundations of the social order in some cases led to disorder. For instance, through evangelical attacks on some beliefs such as the Eyal Odudul and other rites, certain taboos in the community that forbids the killing and eating of the shark and the pouring of ash dust into the river, annual veneration of certain deities, in the community, etc, that held the people together, Christian teaching helped to destroy the fabric of Iduma society[19]. It has been argued that throughout the Niger Delta, the missionaries were largely responsible for the devaluation of the socio—cultural and religious institutions and the world views that sustained them[20]. Operating via their various converts, the missionaries succeeded in undermining the ritual basis of social control in Iduma.

6.4 Economy and Society

The involvement of more people in the Palm oil trade, coupled with the introduction of a new monetary system, produced certain changes in the society. One

19. Punch newspaper, Oct 15th, 2016. Vol 7352, pp 34 – 35

20. Waibinte E. Wariboko, op. cit. page 119

aspect of this monetization of the economy was the imposition of taxes and insistence on payment of these taxes with the European influences. This new development inevitably pushed so many people to produce more for sale and society became more fiercely competitive.

In addition, this development made Houses with very small members and large acreages of land decide no longer to give out their land without payments to other family members of other Houses and resorted to collecting money from them. The Head of such Houses eventually ended up accumulating capital which enabled them to build decent houses of corrugated iron sheets. Moreso, those who became prosperous in the trade became very vocal in the village Assembly and were highly respected. Tradition recounts of such names such as Ikio and Ogolom and a few others.

Nonetheless, the concentrations of wealth in the hands of a few individuals did not result to the emergence of a new type of political leadership or office. And the traditional system of government still remained in the hands of the King (Olilaema), and the House heads (Ikei-Otu).

The introduction of the monetary system brought new policies all over Nigeria. Here in Iduma, the policy of the government to undertake tax collection through the king set some obstruction especially from those who could not pay up. Significantly, also the monetary system offered some explanations of the attractions of some people to the wage economy.

CHAPTER 7
IDUMA AFTER NIGERIA'S INDEPENDENCE
(1960 – 1996)

Introduction

At independence Nigeria became a federation and thus remained a country. Soon afterwards the battle to consolidate t he legacy of dominance by a section of the country over the rest began with increased intensity.

Already, the political parties that emerged were formed based on tribal rather than national interest and therefore had no unifying effect. It became apparent to most curious Nigerians and non-Nigerian observers that all had not been well with the Federation of Nigeria since independence.

This struggle for political hegemony eventually degenerated into serious crisis which led to a coup d'etat and a bloody 30-month civil war with attendant consequences. The Military become more interested in politics rather than its primary constitutional role. The discovery of oil in commercial quantity in Oloibiri, coupled with the oil boom affected the agricultural sector adversely. The economy became heavily dependent on oil for its foreign exchange earnings.

This chapter therefore seeks to examine against this background, the political developments and the socio-economic changes in Iduma during the period. It will also examine the impact of the Nigeria Civil War (Biafran War) and prolonged military rule and general impact on Iduma. However, in our effort to examine the political developments in Iduma within the period, clarity will be promoted in the discussion by first taking a detour to examine briefly the political developments in Nigeria.

7.1 Political Developments in Nigeria (1960-1996)

Nigeria is a pluralistic Nation – State that started as a federation of three political regions at independence in October 1 960[1], and later to four regions. To discuss the political developments in Nigeria in the post- independence era, we will be better off in the discussions, by first examining the events preceding independence in Nigeria, and by taking the post-independence events in phases. I will attempt to do this in four phases as follows:

Phase 1	-	1960 - 1970	- Post-Independence/Nigeria Crisis
Phase 2	-	1970 - 1979	- The Continuity of Military in Politics
Phase 3	-	1979 - 1983	- The Presidential System Experiment

---

1. See Attahiru M. Jega, "The Political Economy of Nigerian Federalism"
in "Foundations of Nigerian Federalism 1960 – 1995," (eds). J. I.
Elaigwu and R. A. Akindele, IGSR, Jos, (2001), page 87.

Phase 4   -   1984 - 1996   -Entrenched Military Rule & Culture

As stated earlier, Nigeria became a federation of three re gions at independence, Professor J. I. Elaigwu defined federalis m essentially as a mechanism for managing conflicts in a multi-cultural state between two types of self-determination - national self-determination which guarantees security for all in the nati on-state on the
one hand, and the self-determination of component
groups to retain their identities on the other hand[2]. He went on to illustrate this by stating that in a federal system of governme nt where there are at least two levels of government, one of whi ch is the central authority and the other the sub-national units. The central represents the whole in matter of national "central" or "common" interest such as defence, foreign affairs, overseas t rade etc, which the other the sub-national units exercise powers of legislation and administration on matters of 'local' or partic

---

[2] See J. I. Elaigwu, "Military Rule and Federalism" in foundations of

Nigerian federalism 1960 – 1995, (eds) J. I. Elaigwu and R. A. Aki ndele,
IGSR, Jos, (2001) page 166

ular interest within the spheres allotted to them by the constitution.

The Nigerian Federation falls within the category of multi-cultural or national State. The regions being the initial federating units, and later replaced by the various States.

A survey of the situation preceding independence reveals some indication that did not promote statehood and nation-building. The growth of nationalism and the subsequent emergence of political parties had tribal inclinations and interests, rather than national interest. Ethnic nationalism was promoted at the expense of national cohesion.

Ethnic movements founded as cultural and welfare associations were transformed into political parties. For instance, the Jam'lyyar Mutanem Arewa founded in 1949 by the Islamic and aristocratic Hausa-Fulani tribes of Northern Nigeria became the nucleus through which the Northern Peoples Congress (NPC) became a political party in 1957, while the Egbe Omo Oduduwa, or descendents of Oduduwa, formed in 1945 transformed into the Action Group (AG). When the National Council of Nigeria and the Cameroons (NCNC) was inaugurated in 1944, the Igbo Union of Lagos became the party's greatest source of support. Though each of these parties had national objectives in varyin g degrees, the interest of the major ethnic groups remained paramount[3].

Minority groups who had entertained fears of likely domination and marginalization at the eve of independence which led to the appointment of a four man commission of enquiry headed by Sir Henry Willink did not also rest on their oars. The Willinks Commission was set up by the colonial government "to ascertain the fact about the fears of Minorities in any part of Nigeria and to propose means of allaying those fears whether well or ill- founded[4]".

The Minority groups also schemed for their political relevance and survival by also forming associations since the major tribal groups appeared to have dominated the predominant political organizations. This may have given vent to the views held by some people to the effect that "Minorities were used by major political parties at home and by other interested outsider po

---

[3] See Ben Naanen, A. I. Pepple, "State Movements" in Land and
 People of Nigeria. Rivers State, (eds) E. J. Alagoa and Tekena N.
 Tamuno, Port Harcourt: Riverside, Communications, (1989), page
 144.
[4] See Henry Willinks et al, op cit.

wers for power juggling exercises during the frequent political c rises in the country[5]. How true this claim is remains a matter for further research, which does not concern me here.

However, a fact that remains indisputable was that in the Niger Delta, a Rivers Peoples League (RPL) was founded in 1941, and later the Rivers Chiefs and People's Conference (RCPC) in 1951 which laid the strong foundation on which the Niger Delta Congress (NDC) was formed on 7th March, 1957[6]. The NDC led by Chief Harold Dappa-Biriye remained the political wing of the Rivers Chiefs and Peoples Conference. The main objective of both the RPL and RCPC being the removal of Rivers territory from Owerri Province as a response to the emerging pattern of domination, and also due to the peculiar terrain of the Niger Delta[7].

---

[5] See Alexander A. Madiebo, The Nigerian Revolution and the Biafra
   War, Enugu: Fourth Dimension Publishers, (1980), page 5.
[6] See Ambily Etekpe et al, "Harold Dappa-Biriye His contribution to
   politics in Nigeria, ed. E. J. Alagoa, Port Harcourt, Onyoma Research, Publications, (2004), Pages 29 - 30.

[7] Ibid, page 29.

Similarly, in the Northern Region, a voice also came out from the middle Belt, where a political party called the United Middle Belt Congress (UMBC) led by Joseph Tarka a Tiv, was founded to spearhead the struggle for Middle Belt State.

I have attempted by this survey to present the picture of the state of affairs in Nigeria at the eve of independence, being the phase before independence.

Post-Independence/Nigeria Crisis (1960 – 1970):

Nigeria gained independence from her colonial master – Great Britain in 1960, and only became a republic in 1963. Queen Elizabeth II was Head of State from October 1, 1960 – October 1, 1963, and ruled with a Governor – General and Prime Minister until a republic was declared in 1963.

The First Republic (1963-1966) had Dr. Nnamdi Azikiwe as ceremonial president, and Sir Abubakar Tafawa Balewa as Prime Minister. This phase (1960 – 1963) was generally characterised by intra and inter party antagonism and tribal jingoists which precipitated the military coups and counter coups and ended in a civil war, with lessons learnt.

Soon after independence, the antagonism against each other and the battle for the legacy of political and to some extent military dominance by one section of the federation over the rest became intensified[8].

It turned out to be a paradox as the people themselves became victims of the political power struggles, which were aimed at removing foreign domination. The wobbly state of affairs which became manifest after the celebration of self rule meant that the situation, instead of improving, deteriorated, as a series of events occurred in quick succession, testing the strength of Nigeria's nationhood.

Firstly, was the Western Nigeria crisis of 1962, which provided the first link in the chain[9]. Chief Samuel L. Akintola, the premier of Western Nigeria had earlier in the year been expelled from the Action Group (AG) for his alleged anti-party activities with the Northern Peoples Congress (NPC), and the Sardauna. He was replaced by Chief Adegbenro. The confused situation that followed disorganized the Action Group, and neutralized Chief Obafemi Awolowo, especially with the formation of the

---

[8] See Alexander A. Madiebo, op. cit. page 4.

[9] See Okay Achike, Ground work of Military Law and Military Rule in
     Nigeria, Enugu, Fourth Dimension, Publishers, (1980), page 93.

NNDP as opposition party to the A.G. calculated to put Chief Awolowo's influence on check in the Western Region.

On 29th May, 1962, when the new Western House of Assembly met and were about to begin the business of the day, supporters of the opposition, NNDP, rose from their seats and began a weird dance on the floor of the House.

One of the dancers seized the Mace, danced towards the Speaker, Prince Adedoyin, took aim at him, missing, and broke the Mace on his table. This led to a confused state, and following this incident, a state of emergency was declared in the Western Region by the Federal Prime Minister, Sir Abubakar Tafawa Balewa, who appointed Dr. Majekodunmi the then Federal Minister of health as Sole Administrator of the Region. The Nigerian Army moved in to enforce the emergency[10].

The second in the link was the population census fiasco of 1963[11].

The population census was intended to furnish the relevant statistics for the distribution of people in the country. The Regional Premiers were vocal in criticizing the alleged rigging of the returns by rival political parties. Although the census figure

---

[10] See Alexander A. Madiebo, (Supra), page 6.
[11] Okay Achike (Supra), Page 93.

s were finally accepted after much rancour, suspicions and ill feelings.

Thirdly, in quick succession, was the federal election. The tension created by the disturbances in western Nigeria and the trials that followed, were still fresh in the minds of many and while the census palaver of 1963 had not completely settled down, the federal election became due in 1964.

Due to allegations of gross election malpractices, some alliances were formed and the Eastern Regional Government was forced to, rather consciously, boycott the elections and control the Federal Parliament. For instance, the Sardauna's NPC merged with S. L. Akintola's NNDP to form the Nigeria National Alliance NNA. In desperation, the NCNC and the AG came into alliance which gave birth to a party called United Progressive Grand Alliance (UPGA).

At last when this Federal election was conducted in October 1965, it became an expensive political exercise that ended in a fiasco, due to the unprecedented rigging; several persons were arrested for election offences. The outcome of the election led to a confrontation between the leaders of rival political parties. For instance, the confrontation between Nigeria's Governor – General, Dr. Nnamdi Azikiwe and the Federal Prime Minister,

Sir Abubakar Tafawa Balewa. Although the election was ultimately compromised after a protracted dialogue, that was not achieved without a price. It created a deep crack in the fibre of Nigerian Unity and Progress.

The Federal Government's decision to accept the results of this election which were entirely rejected by the opposition UPGA angered the people, especially those from the Western Region who suddenly realized that they had lost an opportunity under the constitution of getting a government of their choice in the Region. They may have also realized that the Federal Government was unlikely to shift its stand on the issue. The ultimate result was the outbreak of rioting and violence throughout the Region.

Since independence, corruption, and inefficient administration became the order of the day. Tribalism, nepotism and other societal vices took center-stage. To crown it all, the rigged election in the Western Region in October 1965 and consequential breakdown of law and order precipitated the scheme for military intervention in Nigerian politics.

The foregoing were some of the reasons that led to the event of 15th January 1966 when a group of young army officers led by Major Chukwuma Kaduna Nzeogwu staged a coup d'etat killing in the process, leading politicians and senior military of ficers. Among the politicians killed were Sir Ahmadu Bello, the Sardauna of Sokoto and leader of the North, Chief Samuel L. A kintola leader of the West, Chief Festus Okotie-Eboh, Minister of Finance, and Alhaji Abubakar Tafawa Balewa the Federal Prime Minister. Nzeogwu and his group not having real control of the country, soon surrendered to Major General Johnson Aguiyi-Ironsi who became Head of State[12]. In the East only one senior military officer, Lt. Col. Unegbe was killed. This gave rise to suspicion that since the leader of the coup was an Igbo, it was an Igbo agenda for a bid to power.

On 24th May 1966, General Aguiyi-Ironsi abolished the Regions by promulgating decree No. 34, thus placing the country under a unitary system of government[13]. This act of the Federal Government was greeted with fear and suspicion especially by the northern part which promptly reacted violently and led to the death of several Igbos in the north.

---

[12] See Elechi Amadi and Opubo E. Daminabo, "The Nigerian Civl War" in Land and People of Nigeria; Rivers State, eds, E. J. Alagoa and T. N. Tamuno, Port Harcourt: (1989), page 153.

[13] Elechi Amadi (supra), page 153

In July, 1966 a counter coup led principally by northern army officers was staged, in which General Aguiyi-Ironsi was killed and his government overthrown, and Lt. Col. Yakubu Gowon, a northerner, became Head of State[14].

There arose tension in the country especially between the Igbos led by Lt. Col. Ojukwu, the Governor of the Eastern Region, and Lt. Col. Yakubu Gowon, seen by the Igbos as symbolizing the north. Lt Col. Odumegwu Ojukwu refused to accept his (Gowon) leadership of Nigeria arguing that he was of the same rank with him and he could not be subordinated to him on point of principle the most senior officer of the Army Brigadier Ogundipe ought to be the right person to have succeeded General Aguiyi-Ironsi[15].

All attempts made at reconciliation, including the famous Aburi meeting held between January 4-5, 1967, at

---

[14] Ibid.
[15] See Charles Ogan, Alfred Diete-Spiff, A Legacy of Development
in the Niger Delta, Port Harcourt: (2012) Page 41.
[16] Chinua Achebe, There was a Country: A personal History of
Biafra, Great Britian: Allen Lane, (2012), page. 12
[17] Ibid, page 95

the instance of General Joseph Arthur Ankrah in Ghana to discuss the areas of conflict failed[16].

The Aburi meeting according to Chinua Achebe inspired great optimism as "The instrument to bring lasting peace to Nigeria"[17]. Aburi, in Ghana, was chosen as the venue, as a concession to Ojukwu, who had asked for a neutral venue outside Nigeria for the meeting, but

also to impart a sense of impartiality and credibility to the summit. A document memorializing the areas of shared understanding was produced after two days of meetings, known as the Aburi Accord. The agreement reached raised the hopes of settlement but such hopes of settlement were shattered when both parties returned to Nigeria and gave different interpretations to the agreement reached.

The disagreement detoriated so that on 27 May 1967 in a bid to weaken Lt. Col. Ojukwu, the Head of State promulgated a decree dividing Nigeria into 12 States [18]. Rivers State was one of the States created, which led to the appointment of Lt. Alfred

---

[18] See Arthur A. Nwankwo, Nigeria: The challenge of Biafra, Enugu:
(1972), page 12

Papapreye Diete-Spiff on Sunday 28th May, 1967 as Governor of the newly created State[19]. On 30th May, 1967 Lt. Col. Ojukwu declared secession of the Eastern Region, and proclaimed the independent state of Biafra[20].

A civil war therefore broke out between the Federal Republic of Nigeria and the (secessionist) State of Biafra on 6th July 1967 and ended on 12th January, 1970[21].

Continuity of the Military in Politics (1970 – 1979):
The second segment which I called the phase of continuity of the military in politics witnessed a minimum of three military coups d'etat, including the one that brought in General Yakubu Gowon as Head of State. The others are:
General Murtala Mohammed (1975 – 1976), General Olusegun Obasanjo (1976 – 1979).

At the end of the civil war, in the early 1970s, General Gowon's administration embarked on a programme aimed at re-uniting the people of Nigeria. He therefore introduced the three (3) R.R.R.s as a cardinal policy, which stands for Reconstructio

---

[19] See Charles Ogan, op. cit, page 56.
[20] Arthur A. Nwankwo, (Supra). Page 12
[21] Ibid.

n, Rehabilitation and Reconciliation respectively. The Biafra secessionists capitulated in January 1970. During the 1970s, major reconstruction of the areas that were formally part of Biafra was undertaken.

General Yakubu Gowon added to his credit as the leader, in addition to the creation of 12 States aimed at political stability was the one who ended the Nigerian Civil War and declared that the war had "No victor, no vanquished". Military rule continued and he established the National Youth Service Corps programme as an instrument of national cohesion and unity. The programme afforded young school leavers to serve in any part of the country.

General Yakubu Gowon once said "The trouble with military rule is that every colonel or general is soon full of ambition. The navy takes over today and the army tomorrow[22]. No wonder General Yakubu Gowon's regime was in a matter of time, over thrown on the 29th of July, 1975 and General Murtala Mohammed installed as Head of State.

---

[22] See htt.p://www.dawodu.com/omigui38.htm.acessed on 14th November, 2016

The Murtala regime took a tough stand on indiscipline. It created the Federal Capital Territory, Abuja as Nigeria's new capital after Lagos.

It also created seven (7) more states bringing the total number to 19 and renamed them by removing references to their geographical location. The regime pursued a dynamic foreign policy that was Africa Centric.

He said:
"Africa has come of age; it's no longer under the orbit of any extra continental power. It should no longer take orders from any country, no matter how powerful. Gone are the days when Africa bowed to the threat of any so-called superpowers"[23].

General Murtala Mohammed could not handover power to a democratically elected government before his regime was toppled by some ambitious officers in the military led by Major General B. Dimka and he was assassinated on 13the February, 1976 in the process. This led to the emergence of General Olusegun Obasanjo as Head of State.

---

[23] Cited in Premium Times, February 15, 2016

General Obasanjo continued with the policy thrust of the Murtala government, hence most writers had often referred to that regime as Murtala/Obasanjo regime.

General Obasanjo inaugurated the Constituent Assembly that resulted in the promulgation of the 1979 Constitution. He was the first Nigeria Head of State to hand over power willingly. Thus he had said in several fora that when he left office in 1979, he was about the only one who really left office of his own accord.

The Presidential System Experiment (1979 – 1983):

This takes us to the third phase; 1979-1983, which I have called The Presidential System Experiment.

This phase is widely known in Nigerian political history as the Second Republic. In this study I called it the phase of presidential experiment due to the way the Shagari government was hurriedly overthrown by the military. The military had always brought themselves into power with the excuse of being on a "redemption mission" which had never been its real intentions.

The Shehu Shagari government though short-lived, was known for its ideals as an administration that promoted true democracy, in conduct and general relationship with the other tiers and arms of government. Shehu Shagari was a champion of democracy.

By the overthrow of this regime by the military on 31st December, 1983 on alleged corruption, election rigging and general misrule, etc, this phase was terminated.

Entrenched Military Rule and Culture (1984 – 1996):

The phase of entrenched military rule and culture started in 1984 and ended in 1996. The first beneficiary of this phase from the military circle was General Muhammadu Buhari (1984 – 1985). He promised to return the country to civil rule after the restoration of normalcy, but he could not before he was overthrown and detained by General Ibrahim B. Babangida.

The Buhari government introduced the "War Against Indiscipline", and this was the hallmark of the Buhari administration. He was known to be incorruptible and championed anti-corruption crusades. The Buhari government was yet to stabilize when a clique of army officers organized a coup d'etat, which some described as a palace coup; in the process he was ousted and Major General Ibrahim Babangida emerged as the new helm sman and took the name of President and Commander-in-Chief of the Armed Forces.

As usual as with most military rules, he promised to return the country to civilian rule within the shortest time but he never did. He introduced the option A4 voting system and open ballot system as part of his election reforms. He approved two political parties for the government – the National Republican Convention (NRC) and Social Democratic Party (SDP).

He created additional states, bringing the total number to 30. He promised to hand over power but ended up with the longest transition to Civil Rule Programme, which he had no faith in, hence on June 12th he annulled that election result that was considered the fairest in the history of the country. He resigned and handed over the reins of government to Chief Ernest Shonekan, a civilian, on August 26th, 1993 as Head of the Interim National Government, ostensibly leaving General Sani Abacha behind as the real strong man being the one who called the shots in that brief period.

Ernest Shonekan was in charge from August 26 – November 17, 1993. This short period was known as the Third Republic in Nigeria's political history. The Head of Government at the federal level and the Ministers were appointed but at the State l evel, the governors and members of the various State Houses of Assembly were elected. There were also elected officers at the l ocal government area level. This arrangement became apparent due to the annulment of the election conducted on June 12 whic h produced Chief Moshood Abiola and Ambassador Babagana Kingibe respectively, as presidential and vice-presidential candi dates who were the presumed winners of the June 12, 1993 pres idential election, but were not sworn in until the Shonekan-led f ederal government was overthrown by General Sani Abacha on November 17, 1993.

On assumption of office, General Abacha dismantled all democratic structures in the country and appointed Military Ad ministrators to all the States of the Federation and Major Gener al Oladipo Diya was appointed the Chief of General Staff (CGS) . The administration also followed its predecessors in aspects of constitutional suspension and modifications. It suspended the 1989 and the Interim National Government (ING) Constitution and returned the country to a modified 1979 Constitution[24].

In 1994 in a bid to reclaim his mandate on the June 12 19 93 elections which he won with 58% votes across the country, A

---

[24] See J. I. Elaigwu, op. cit. Page 181

lhaji Moshood Abiola was arrested, detained and charged with treason for declaring himself President.

Professor Wole Soyinka, winner of the 1986 Nobel Prize for literature and other eminent Nigerians fled Nigeria for their lives for being critical of the Abacha regime. General Abacha came to be widely known as the maximum ruler due to his dictatorial and crude form of all-military rulership.

In October, 1995 General Abacha promised to step down in three years after reforms were complete.

General Abacha became more daring as in the same year the military government hanged nine (9) political activists in November, including well-known playwright, and environmental activist Kenule Saro-Wiwa who was accused of involvement in the killings of four (4) pro-government traditional chiefs from Ogoni in 1994. This led to the suspension of Nigeria from the Commonwealth of Nations, a reputable organization for Britain and her former colonies.

On 1st October, 1996 in a national television broadcast General Abacha announced the creation of additional six (6) States, including Bayelsa State thus bringing the total number to 36.

On June 8, 1998 General Abacha died at his villa in Abuja, with no sign of previous ill-health. He was quickly replaced by a close ally, Major General Abdulsalami Alhaji Abubakar.

The death of General Abacha signaled the end of the era of maximum dictatorship often referred to as the dark days of Nigeria political history but not the end of military rule in Nigeria. The regime was known within and outside Nigeria as the worst with respect to human rights abuses and several other atrocities. Hence, General Abacha remains the most vilified Nigerian Head of State even at death.

The Abacha experience remains a "must learn lesson" for all those in leadership positions, and those aspiring for leadership positions, especially those in Africa, as the legacy created by our style of leadership out-lives us as mortals.

7.2 Political Developments in Iduma

Here, in Iduma as earlier stated, the news of granting of formal independence to Nigeria on 1st October, 1960 was received with great joy and jubilation. Elections were over, and the politicians who made several promises on the platform of their respective political parties during the campaigns had since disappeared as vapour.

Having little or no voice at local, state and the federal levels, they had no choice than to turn their attention once more to their traditional institutions of town government, and look forward to better prospects in the future.

The early sixties also turned out to be a phase of much challenges both at home and the wider world. In particular, the year 1963 was very turbulent and gloomy. It was the year the population census figures nearly tore the nation apart due to the dispute that arose out of the final figures of that census which returns were said to have been rigged in certain area. Just as this controversy was beginning to die down, the sad news of the death of HRH King Abiosi Adewari, Igoniwari the XI, Olilaema of Idema filtered into town. In the words of an elder "The late King Abiosi had been a very good ruler of the community and was known for his good candour and art of diplomacy in community matters"[25].

The announcement of the death of a King in Iduma following a successful oracle test (Odol), was usually greeted with a thunderous communal "Ogele" dance and the slaughtering of domestic animals including harvesting of plantain found in the community. This was undertaken as a demonstration that the King owns all in the community.

---

[25] Mr. Stanley Burufegha, circac. 74 years, personal interview, Idema, 25/03/90

As tradition demanded, at the death of a King in Iduma, following his formal burial, the oracle (Odol) of the deceased in consultation with the ancestors gave sanctions to the appointment of a regent within the Ebo lineage. Following this procedure, Chief Oke Benson Garrick was appointed Regent of Idema in 1963.

The final burial rites of the late King Abiosi Adewari was yet to be concluded when the news about the political upheavals in the country became localized. It then became a topic of daily discussion in most public places. The situation in the western region was said to have detoriated, occasioned by the rigged federal elections conducted in October 1965, and the resultant violence that ensued. Fear had gripped most villagers due to the heightened tension in the country.

The news of the Nzeogwu-led coup d'etat of 15th January, 1966 had hit the town, and not too long after, information about the July 29, 1966 Coup organized principally by Northern elements that ushered in Yakubu Gowon was rife.

The Igbo elements in the community were also very apprehensive, especially when the news broke out that General Johnson Aguiyi-Ironsi had been killed, alongside with other Igbos. Again, that Odumegwu Ojukwu had threatened to secede from the federation of Nigeria with the Eastern Region.

However, the creation of Rivers State on 27th May, 1967 by the Head of State Lt. Yakubu Gowon along with other eleven states in the federation, and the subsequent appointment of Lt. Alfred Diete-Spiff the following day brought joy to Iduma[26]. An exercise some scholars have argued was designed to alienate the ethnic minorities of Eastern Region from Biafran secession and secure the support of the Middle Belt groups for the federal war effort[27].

The good news about the creation of Rivers State by the federal military government, and the appointment of a Nembe man as Governor became determinant factors on whose side of the divide Iduma would align to in the crisis. Though, Rivers State was created, and a Governor appointed, the young Governor Lt. A. P. Diete-Spiff, could not immediately assume office because by that time Ojukwu had sealed off the Eastern Region from the rest of the country, which made it impossible for most people in Rivers State including Iduma to move to Por

---

[26] Charles Ogan, (supra), page 56
[27] Okwudibia Nnoli, 'Ethnic and Regional Balancing in Nigerian
Federalism' in "Foundations Of Nigeria Federalism 1960 – 1995",
eds. J. I. Elaigwu and R. A. Akindele, Jos: IGSR, (2001), pages 223

t Harcourt. It was not until September 1968 when the greater part of Rivers State had been liberated that the Governor was able to move to Port Harcourt[28].

One event that angered Iduma, to have developed hatred against Ojukwu and his Biafra secession bid was the destruction of two of its communities, Idema and Eboh on 16th May, 1968, by a contingent of Biafra troops based in Kugbo.

This event emboldened young men in the community and gave them impetus to enlist into the federal forces against Biafra.

By September 1968 Chief Garrick's rulership came under threat. Chief Garrick organized soldiers from Okoroba, a neighbouring community, and subjected elders of the Ebo group of Houses to public odium, by instructing the said federal soldiers to flog the elders in the Community Hall where primary school pupils were invited to record the cane count.

The reason behind the action of the regent was unconnected with a leaked plot to remove him from office. He then quickly resorted to the use of the federal soldiers who were then at Okoroba to intervene.

---

[28] Charles Ogan, (op cit), page 56 and 56

As events unfolded, the intervention appeared temporary, as no sooner than the soldiers left Iduma to Okoroba the plot to unseat him as Regent thickened. The aggrieved Ebo Elders perfected their strategy and summoned an enlarged family meeting where a vote of no confidence was passed on Chief Garrick for high handedness. Hence, he was unanimously deposed as the Regent of Idema and replaced by Elder Egiri Young Jack Ofere. The new Regent was thereafter presented to the Idema community.

The new Regent, ruled over Idema in the remaining part of the Nigerian civil war era and after. He showed commitment and dedication in leadership, in spite of the serious handicap of not being educated.

At creation, Rivers State comprised five (5) administrative divisions and seventeen (17) county councils established under the Eastern Nigeria Local Government Law No. 17 of 1960[29]. The Brass Division comprised the following county councils:

    i.   Nembe County Council
    ii.   Ogbia County Council
    iii.   Southern Ijaw County Council

---

[29] Ibid, page 108

iv. Northern Ijaw County Council

These county councils were dissolved during the military coup of 1966. They were however, resuscitated by a subsequent edict after the creation of Rivers State. The Interim Local Government Councils Edict No. 5 of 1969 was promulgated re-establishing the former councils [30].

At the end of the Civil War, a variety of experiments were tried on the running of local government system by the state government. This was made possible by the Gowon-led military government's liberal policy, by allowing state government's to take full responsibility for the system of local government in their respective states.

Under an administrative re-organisation edict of 1973, 18 new administrative divisions were created. All the 17 interim local government councils were dissolved and town/community councils were established. The edict provided for a total of 13

---

[30] See Local Government Administration in Rivers State of Nigeria.
Port Harcourt: Ministry of Information. Also E. W. Appah, Esq,
compilation of Administrative Divisions in the Rivers State, 1969,
pages 10-11

0 town/community councils excluding Port Harcourt which was given a city status[31]. Idema was accorded the status of a principal town and a town council was appointed.

During the Diete-Spiff era, Iduma was till grouped in Nembe County Council of Brass Division, with Twon-Brass as the Divisional Administrative Headquarters. The Iduma communities were grouped into two different local councils – Mini (Abureni) and Oluasiri respectively. For instance, Idema, Eboh, and Obeduma were collectively referred to as Idema and grouped within the Mini (Abureni) Local Council, while other communities such as Emalo, Oboghe (Emiesekiri), Ematadu (Adukiri), Ematande (Odekiri), Ogbomasaga (Sangapiri), Okiroma, Ematabiosi, etc were grouped with other Nembe settlements in the Oluasiri cluster to form the Oluasiri Local Council.

The reason behind this arrangement of splitting the Iduma communities into two local councils could be for administrative convenience as conceived by the early administrators. This is often an excuse easily advanced when an evil act became indefensible. The so-called arrangement rather than improving their participation in local government administration, made them more vulnerable to domination and marginalization.

---

[31] See Charles Ogan, op cit, pages 56 and 66

The Egiri Regency had its own challenges in Idema especially with respect to the handling of displaced persons, and the distribution of relief materials donated by government, during and immediately after the war.

Several family members shared the same residential accommodation, and relief supplies such as garbon garri, stock fish, corrugated iron sheets etc, donated, were often not enough to go round the large population.

In April, 1974 following the appointment, and subsequent coronation of Mr. Felix Ebutu Aboko as substantive Olilaema of Idema, and Mr. Diegha Inko as his deputy (Ipali Olilaema) the Egiri Regency came to an end.

Mr. Felix E. Aboko was selected for the office of Olilaema from his maternal Aloki-Obodiri royal lineage in accordance with Iduma tradition. This became possible due to the inability of two other royal lineages – Ikpoku and Ogu to present suitable candidates. Though Ogu presented a candidate that was later discovered to be unsuitable and was accordingly rejected; the choiced candidate from Ikpoku, Mr. Edward Odu declined the offer and went into hiding. Hence, both lineages were foreclosed before the process moved to the Obodiri Group of Houses, from where Mr. Felix E. Aboko was opportuned to be appointed from the Aloki axis of Obodiri Royal House. Similarly, Mr. Diegha

Inko, the candidate for the Deputy Olilaema was also appointed from his maternal lineage of Ebo. His appointment came from the Adiboko axis of Ebo House. The Ebo Group of Houses comprise Eme and Adiboko 'Houses' the rightful lineages for the position of deputy Olilaemaship, and
regency in Idema according to Iduma tradition[32].

In 1976, there were attempts to reform the local government system in the country which brought about a unified local government system in Nigeria. This was done in preparation for local government elections in the subsequent year. When the local government elections were held throughout the federation, one Chief Christopher Abu also contested in that election. He contested for the office of councillor, under the Mini (Abureni) Local Council. The Iduma candidate, Chief Christopher Abu was roundly defeated in the said election for reasons unconnected with the fragmentation of his political base into two local counc

---

[32] See Local Government Administration in Rivers State of Nigeria.
Port Harcourt: Ministry of Information. Also E. W. Appah, Esq.
compilation of Administrative Divisions in the Rivers State, 1969,
pages 10 - 11

ils. In the circumstance, he could not garner enough votes to be elected. Iduma once again slumped into political oblivion, confirming the fears earlier expressed with respect to the danger in the balkanization of Iduma villages into two local councils.

In 1979, following the election of Chief Melford Obiene Okilo as Governor of Rivers State, the government set up the Ateli commission to look into the question of reforming of local government arrangements in the state. This was with a view to bringing about greater efficiency in local government administration.

The Iduma and the rest of Abureni made strong representation demanding for a separate Abureni District Council for all Abureni communities in the then Brass and Degema Local Government Areas[33].

The Rivers State Government could not grant Iduma and the rest of Abureni their demand, perhaps for reasons that the communities were not in one local government area. However, it created Emago/Amuruto Urban Council for the Kugbos, under Degema Local Government Area, and merged Akani, one of the Abureni communities with the Oduals. All the Iduma com

---

[33] Informant: Chief John I. Ebifa Adiboko, former regent of Idema, 78
years, Idema, 25/07/2008

munities including Agrisaba, and Okoroba formally of the Nembe District were transferred to an omnibus Ogbia District within the then Brass Local Government Area[34]. Thus ended over 80 years of Nembe (Bassambiri) domination of Iduma and the rest of Abureni in local government.

This may have brought some relief to Iduma and the rest of Abureni, as they were certainly opened to more opportunities, in spite of the fact that their ultimate desire was not met.

Following the transfer of Iduma and the rest Abureni villages from Nembe District to Ogbia District, two separate electoral wards were created. Ward 23 comprising Agrisaba and Okoroba, and Ward 24 comprising Idema I, Idema II (Obeduma) and Eboh[35].

This new arrangement was to give political relevance to these communities since they were able to elect their representatives into the various wards. Apart from this, several Iduma indigenes were opportuned to be appointed by the Okilo administr

---

[34] See Rivers State Local Governments Law, 1980 (No. 4 of 1981), and
 supplement to Rivers State of Nigeria official Gazette No. 16, vol.
 15, 25/07/1983, B. 76

[35] See R. S. L. V. No. 11 of 1983 – Delimitation of wards Order. B. 75

ation into functional committees at the Ogbia District level, under the State Government's decentralization policy.

However, the military coup d'etat that brought in Major – General Muhammadu Buhari as Head of State, and Brigadier General Tunde Idiagbon as Chief of General Staff Supreme Headquarters led to several other changes in the structure of local government administration. As is the case with military governments, the 1979 Constitution was suspended and modified to give room for rulership by decree[36].

The federal military government hurriedly appointed state governors to all the states of the federation. Mr. Fidelis Oyakhilome was appointed Governor of Rivers State. Upon assumption of office he dissolved all the functional committees, including the districts, urban councils, and electoral wards etc and ordered a reversal to the status quo. Thus, all the Abureni communities earlier transferred to Ogbia District were reverted to Nembe District, of the Old Brass Local Government Area. The entire Brass Local Government Area was delimited into twelve Electoral Wards. Iduma and the rest Abureni towns/villages includin

---

[36] See the Constitution (suspension and modification) Decree No. 1
of 1984

g the Nembe settlements in Ikensi and Oluasiri were constituted into one ward (ie Brass ward 5).

The arrangement however, did not give Iduma the opportunity of fair representation at the Brass Local Government Council either by direct election or appointment.

The report of the 21-member committee appointed by the Buhari Military administration of 1983 – 1985, otherwise known as the Dasuki Report was to bring about much improvement to the local government system. This Report was submitted in 1985, but the Buhari administration could do very little work with it before it was overthrown.

The Political Bureau which the Babangida administration appointed in January 1986 to search for a viable political future for Nigeria, among other things, endorsed many of the recommendations of the Dasuki Report, including retaining the 301 Local Government one-tier system of 1976 – 1979. Of particular interest was government acceptance to retain the 301 multi-purpose local government areas and to establish within each local government council, a minimum of five Development Area Centres in May 1987.

In the then Brass Local Government Area, seven Development Area Centres were created[37]. The sub-units for the Brass Local Government Area and the designated centres were: (1) Akassa with Akassa as centre, (2) Brass/Okpoma with Okpoma as centre, (3) Oluasiri/Idema with Idema as centre, (4) Ogbia with Ogbia Town as Centre, (5) Emeyal with Emeyal as centre, (6) Anyama with Anyama as centre, (7) Okoroma with Ologoma as centre.

Unfortunately, the Dasuki Report was yet to be implemented when the Babangida administration by May 1989 created 149 new local government areas throughout the federation, thus bringing the total number to 589, and the Area Development Centres could not be implemented.

The creation of more states and local government areas in 1991 brought about new centres of growth and development in the country. In that exercise, the Brass Local Government Area was split into two, with the Ogbia District constituting a new local government area.

The Iduma people had expressed their desire to be part of the Ogbia local government area prior to its creation. When it was finally created and Iduma was not part of it, the communit

---

[37] See Nigerian Tide of Thursday, January 26, 1989, page 1

y sent various petitions to relevant quarters including the offices of the Governor and Deputy Governor of Rivers State.

After all these representations - especially the one to the State government - had failed, they embarked on a public protest on 25th November, 1991, on the streets of Port Harcourt. In the course of their protest, they succeeded in intercepting the convoy of the Military Governor of Rivers State, - Governor Godwin Abbe at the UTC junction area in Port Harcourt City.

Upon sighting the protesting group, the Governor stopped his convoy and demanded to know the reason for the protest, and having listened to the group he said "The Iduma people have the right to choose where they belong and it is not the place of government to stand against their legitimate desire"[38]. Having said that he immediately approved the transfer of all Iduma communities in Nembe District of the Old Brass LGA to Ogbia Local Government Area. He also directed the comptroller of the National Population Commission, Rivers State, to ensure that in the forth- coming National Census, all Iduma communities sho

---

[38] This statement is credited to Colonel Godwin Abbe, Military Administrator, Rivers State when he granted the request of the Iduma people's transfer from Nembe District, Brass LGA, to Ogbia

Local Government Area during the public protest led by the author on 25/11/1991, in Port Harcourt.

uld be enumerated in Ogbia Local Government Area, for proper integration. This is how Iduma towns/villages of the Abureni clan with the exception of Okoroba and Agrisaba finally escaped from Nembe (Bassambiri) domination for over nine decades.

The wise decision of the Military Governor, no doubt brought joy to all Iduma at home and in the diaspora. Hence, 25th November of every year had been set aside as Jubilee Day, and is being celebrated in remembrance of that event.

Following, the official transfer of Iduma towns/villages into Ogbia Local Government Area, an electoral Ward 14 was approved for Iduma on 11th December, 1991, with collation centre at Obeduma[39]. However, occasioned by intrigues and bureaucratic bottle-necks, the file on which that approval was obtained got missing in the Rivers State office of the National Electoral Commission which consequently rendered the approval nugatory.

By 1994 when a Caretaker Committee was to be appointed to run the Ogbia Local Government Council, Capt. Glory Ko

---

[39] See Letter written by the author and other community leaders
dated 4th December 1991 upon which Electoral ward 14 was approved by the National Electoral Commission on 11/12/11.

ru (rtd.), from Iduma was among the five-member management committee appointed for Ogbia. Thus the appointment of Capt. Glory Koru (rtd.) symbolized the first fruit of the struggle for emancipation.

By 1995, the National Electoral Commission embarked on yet another ward delimitation exercise. In that exercise Idema, Obeduma, Eboh, Emalo, Oboghe including other Iduma villages and Ogbia town were constituted into Ogbia Ward 1 with Ogbia town as collation centre. Since the creation of the ward, Iduma sons and daughters have contested and won elections into the local government council, in addition to other appointments.

In furtherance of their quest for some form of autonomy, an Iduma District has since been created, comprising all Iduma villages in the Ogbia Local Government Area, with Iduma City as the district headquarters.

7.3 Economic and Social Changes

At independence in 1960, the Iduma people continued with their main economic activities of fishing and farming alongside other related economic ventures, though, these economic activities thrived, the palm oil and kernel production and logging continued to attract the young and able-bodied due to the income earned by those involved in the business.

The availability of the oil palm tree in Iduma land in large quantity soon became a source of attraction to persons from other lands who came to be involved either as producers, or buyers of the produce or commodities. For instance, the Urhobo (Osobo), and Isoko came as palm cutters and producers, while the Nembes and Kalabaris who came and lived amongst the people were produce buyers. The Urhobos and Isokos initially lived amongst the natives before they later established separate settlements at Ozibh-Onyeke, and Otuogba, and Oghilolo at the outskirts of the community.

The local farmers and fishermen produced enough to feed their families and had surplus for sale from which they earned income. There was relative stability in community life both at the economic and social levels, which continued up to the Nigerian Civil War era.

However, at the end of the Civil War, Iduma began to notice some changes at both the economic and social levels. The changes that were noticed came about as a result of certain fundamental factors. Most importantly were the Nigerian Civil War and the discovery of oil in commercial quantity in Oloibiri in 1958, and the subsequent oil boom in the 70s. I will like to examine firstly, the changes brought about by the Nigerian Civil War. The war had its effect on the palm oil and kernel business. The c ivil war led to general decline in the production of palm oil and kernels in the Eastern Region. This fact is understandable since the entire Eastern Region was like a war theatre during the crisis.

Furthermore, the general hostilities associated with the war did not allow the Iduma people continue with the business of production. The sacking of two of its communities – Idema and Eboh – by the Biafran Forces aggravated the situation since the survivors were compelled to flee for their safety. The war also compelled the non-natives – Nembes, Kalabaris, Urhobos and Isokos at Ozibhonyeke, Oghilolo and Otuogba Camps to desert their camps and flee to their native homes for safety.

Meanwhile, the energetic young men who would have been involved in the productive sector resolved after the sacking of Idema and Eboh to enlist into the Nigerian Army. The rest who did not enlist into the army were attracted to Port Harcourt by the opportunities opened to them in other areas of business and the public service.

The second major factor that affected the decline of the palm oil and kernel production was the discovery of oil in commercial quantity in 1958 at Oloibiri – Ogbia. This development resulted to new opportunities in the petroleum sector. Young and able-bodied men that were involved in the tedious palm oil and kernel production business were attracted to oil exploration and exploitation-related jobs, of which the remuneration and perks of office were relatively better.

Similarly, the oil boom in the 1970s resulting from the Arab oil embargo on the USA in 1973 brought about an adverse effect on the agricultural sector. The nation had cheap money to import all sorts of things including foodstuff manufactured goods etc. the economy witnessed structural changes in the 1980s, attributed to slow growth[40]. Those engaged in palm oil and kernel production and other agro-allied economic activities were consequently affected.

Rural – urban migration increased as people were attracted to reap the benefits from the oil wind-fall. Production of palm oil and kernel and other commodities for local consumption as well as for export declined.

Food production also became a problem as more and more people were attracted to the urban centres for white-collar jobs, and other profitable ventures in the private sector that were not available at Iduma.

---

[40] Afolabi Khadijat, Impact of oil Export on Economic growth in
Nigeria from 1970 – 2006, (2011). unpublished research work

In the larger society, the policies of successive governments in the country were unable to reverse the ugly trend. Despite the oil boom, the private sector remained weak. The existing macroeconomic policies continued to encourage consumption rather than production. The economy was consuming what she was not producing.

In most rural communities including Iduma, imported foodstuff, canned fish, canned meat, including frozen fish (iced fish) were introduced and the people became used to them as part of their regular diet. Genuine efforts were not made by successive governments in improving the traditional fishing and farming methods and techniques to bring about greater productivity and food sufficiency.

Most of the agricultural policies initiated by either the federal or state governments such as the Operation Feed the Nation (OFN) and Green Revolution by the Federal Government, Agrarian Aggressive Agricultural Policy (AAAP) by the Rivers State government, etc were not properly followed through to achieve the desired goals.

Though the introduction of nylon nets and other modern fishing gears was done to dramatically replace the old-fashioned traps and fishing mats, (itata), that were in vogue in the pre-colonial era. Again, the policy of distribution of powered canoe s and modern fishing gears to fishermen, including the supply of fishing co-operatives with modern equipment and cash subsidies was aimed at boosting fish production, and perhaps to check rural – urban drift, but the implementation of the policy, and many others, ended up abysmally in the cities. Most rural dwellers including those in Iduma did not benefit from the policy.

Government did not also encourage the genuine improvement of the old fishing methods and techniques as could be seen from the various policies initiated. For instance in Iduma, the miripaka[41] fishing technique was abandoned by the people due to lack of government encouragement, and the will to improve the technique for the benefit of the people.

The discovery of oil in commercial quantity in the late 1950s and the subsequent oil boom in the 1970s led to the decline of virtually most economic activities ranging from farming, fish

---

[41] "Miripaka" is a form of community fishing done by blocking a section of a creek during full tide so that by the ebb or low tide when the water must have gone down fishes were trapped and villagers took advantage of the low tide and fished within the blocked section. A section of the Iduma creek was usually blocked for it, and was done once in five or more years.

ing, production of raffia products, canoe production to palm oil and kernel production etc.

Dr. Osita Agbu had noted that by the 1970s, oil had become the fiscal basis of the Nigerian state, effectively replacing agriculture as the basis of wealth accumulation in Nigeria[42]. The petro-dollar economy encouraged the mass importation of all sorts of goods into the country which brought about economic changes in most parts of the country including Iduma.

There were also changes at the social level of Iduma society which was sequel to the changes that had taken place in the economic sector. These changes became apparent since the economy is the basis on which the social sector operates.

The changes that took place in the educational sector were initiated by the early Christian missions. For instance, St. Johns' School Idema was established in 1927. Though the school got stagnated at standard four for decades on grounds of low enrolment, this was to change in the coming years, with the growth of awareness of the benefits of Western education.

---

[42] Osita Agbu, "Oil and the National Question in Nigeria: The external Dimension" in Nigerian Journal of International Affairs,
Vol. 26, No. 1, 200, page 102.

In 1972, the Rivers State government acting on the Brass Divisional Educational Authority's recommendation, upgraded the primary school to primary five in the first instance, and subsequently to primary six status by 1973.

By 1975, the Universal Primary Education Scheme (UPE) provided opportunity for more primary schools to be established. Consequently, two additional primary schools were established for Iduma, UPE II Idema and UPE Obeduma respectively. These three primary schools provided the basis for the granting of a college to Iduma in 1980 by the Rivers State Government under Governor Melford Okilo. Thus, the college became the first to be established in Abureni soil. The college provided educational opportunities for Iduma and the rest of Abureni, including the neighbouring Nembe satellite villages of Obiata, Agada, and Atubo II.

All those who went through these schools were exposed to Western ideas and culture. The mode of formal instruction was in the English Language, and very soon it became obvious of the level of transformation that had taken place.

In the same period, the Rivers State Government established a secondary health facility – Cottage Hospital Idema, intended to take care of the health needs of Iduma and the neighbouring villages.

Though, established in 1980, the hospital suffered long abandonment occasioned by the military takeover of government in December, 1983, and other successive governments that were not interested in completing projects embarked upon by the defunct civilian administration. The hospital was eventually taken over by the Niger Delta Development Commission and completed in later years.

The establishment of the hospital brought about social changes in the community. The awareness created by both the federal and state government on the necessity of immunization of children to free them from life-threatening diseases such as polio, measles, hepatitis, etc, was realized by the presence of the health facility, and the personnel deployed to the hospital.

The period also witnessed changes in the transportation sector. The old means of transportation by canoes underwent some transformation. In the early 1960s, the mode of transportation gradually changed to powered Achimedes and Evinrude brand engines especially for giant public transport boats that plied in the community and other places.

Soon after the Nigerian Civil War there were further improvements in the transportation system. Outboard and inboard built engines of the Evinrude brand started plying the Iduma Port Harcourt route. In the 1980s, the Yamaha brand of engine, gradually replaced the earlier engines. Fibre made speed boats, and other giant wooden boats powered by Yamaha engines were introduced and became operational. In the early 1990s, motor cycles became another means of transport, through the first oil well location to Iduma. These changes transformed the public transportation sector.

During the period, there were also changes brought about through cultural mix. Culturally, European forms and patterns of behavior gained ground. The social structure, the thought-system and mode of dress was influenced by both European and other cultures that came into contact with Iduma culture.

Aged old traditions were influenced by these contacts. Although it was usual for these cultural changes to occur because when two cultures meet, the weaker culture was usually subdued by the stronger one, culminating into a change. These changes became so pervasive that some children can hardly communicate in their native language.

Finally, the operation of multi-national corporations such as Shell Petroleum Development Company (SPDC), Nigerian Agip Oil Company (NAOC), etc, in the area, brought about some negative social behaviour by Iduma ladies. The friendly association between these young girls and ladies with the staff of these oil companies exposed them to anti-social behaviour and imm oral attitudes which hitherto was unknown in the society. I am not inclined to list some of these anti-social behaviour as it is nedless doing so because such behaviour has acquired notoriety that is of public knowledge. Moreover it has denigrated Iduma culture.

7.4 Impact of the Nigeria Civil War

As earlier stated, the general lack of concern for the electorates by the politicians of the First Republic, coupled with the increasing violent unrest in the Western Region, were some of the factors which led to the January 15, 1966 coup which brought in Major – General Johnson Aguiyi-Ironsi into power. General Ironsi's attempt to impose a unitary system of government by decree No. 34 of 1966 angered the Northerners which eventually led to the counter Coup of July 29, 1966 that brought in Lt. Col. Yakubu Gowon[43].

When on May 27, 1967 Gowon created 12 States, it was considered as a move to break up the Eastern Region, hence on May 30, 1967, Colonel Ojukwu declared the Eastern Region of Nigeria as an Independent State of Biafra. This was considered a rebellion by the Federal Military Government, who later decla

---

[43] Olusegun Obasanjo, My Command, Ibadan, (1980), page 6

red war on Biafra on July 6, 1967, in an attempt to foil Colonel Odumegwu Ojukwu's secession plan[44].

When the war commenced, Iduma was neutral, as it was yet to come to terms with the reasons behind plunging the nation into war.

However, that neutrality soon ended when on May 16, 1968 two villages in Iduma, Eboh and Idema were burnt down to ashes by the Biafran soldiers for an alleged federal support. Consequently, many people were either killed, wounded and maimed, and others forcefully taken away and detained in the heart of Igbo land, and branded as saboteurs.

A few days to the incident, rumour was rife that Biafran soldiers based in Kugbo were to visit Iduma for undisclosed reasons. This rumour was dismissed as a non-issue, until the invading Biafran forces were sighted from a distance on that fateful day by Mr. Godspower Alabiobio who raised the alarm.

The soldiers were led by three indigenes of Kugbo, Messrs Morrison K. Esadi, Joel Marcus and one Clinton. The whole incident that brought about the invasion was linked to an earlier visit by a contingent of federal troops to Iduma in a bid to track down a certain alleged supporter of Biafra - Mr. Sunday Igbaru

---

[44] Ibid, page 13

ku of Nembe. The said Mr. Igbaruku had secretly sneaked into Iduma and was taking refuge in his lady friend (Miss. Anty Offor's) private home.

During that visit the Nigerian soldiers were said to have fired several gun shots into the air, ostensibly, to register their presence as a signal to wade off perceived enemies. The news of the Nigerian soldiers' visit spread to Kugbo through some Kugbo youths who were at Obeduma during the visit. These Kugbo youths had gone to inform the Biafran soldiers at Kugbo that Iduma was under siege by federal forces.

This story agitated the Biafran soldiers at Kugbo, who insisted that they must visit Iduma, and demanded for escort. As earlier stated, three Kugbo indigenes escorted the soldiers to Iduma.

While I will not want to delve into or comment on the propriety or otherwise of the role of the three Kugbo indigenes, with respect to their indulgence in the trip, the resultant consequences were traumatic. The havoc wrecked by the Biafran soldiers on the innocent civilian population at Iduma left a very bitter experience in the town.

This ugly experience of the war cannot easily be forgotten. In that invasion, men of God were also not spared from brutality. Mr. Stephen Happy, a committed Christian and leader of t he First Baptist Church, Obeduma became the first victim to be shot dead on that day. The deceased left behind him, a wife and several children.

After this atrocity, the survivors deserted the villages to neighbouring places such as Okoroba, Oruan (Atubo I), Oboghe, Emalo, Elemuama (Obokorobo), Iyoize and subsequently suffered great hardships as they had to flee from place to place in search of safety.

The Biafran atrocities and the subsequent mass exodus of the people to other places of abode produced very memorable effects on the lives of the people. Initially, Iduma youths were not keen on enlisting in the army of either side. But with the May 16th incident, there was an abrupt change of heart. Many youths now escaped to enlist in the Nigerian Army with a view either to revenge or to die on the battle field rather than endure misery.

The civil war hampered the economic activities of the people. From the time these communities were razed to ashes it became extremely difficult for people to go about their normal business.

The farmers were to suffer most since their farms especially those located in far away Abua and Odual territories becam e very unsafe for them, and this eventually led people to depend largely on seafood.

Those who could not enlist in the Nigerian Army, and who had no fishing equipment to fish in the creeks or swamps where they lived, resorted to salt manufacturing which was then very lucrative. Others, especially the women, took to trading in salt and dried fish, which they sneaked across the checking points for resale to people on the Biafran side. On their return journey, they brought foodstuff from the Biafran territory for sale to those on the Nigerian side, who were in dire need of food. This business itself was very risky since those discovered were apt to be branded by both sides as saboteurs, after which they would be executed or held as hostages or sometimes detained in terrible cells.

However, by September 1968 the problems of communication and security that hampered the internal movement of people within the Brass area was somehow reduced. This was due largely to the concerted efforts of the federal troops, who combed out all traces of Biafran resistance in the towns and villages. People whose settlements had been burnt down now started returning home.

The civil war also brought about a negative impact on Iduma socially. The incident of 16th May 1968 led to the indefinite closure of the only primary school at Idema. The invasion and consequent destruction of infrastructure rendered the entire community unsafe for academic activities. The school remained closed until the villages were resettled.

The liberation of Port Harcourt by the federal forces in mid May 1968 was to attract a large number of people from the out-lying villages and towns of the state, who saw it as their city. Port Harcourt City was before the war largely dominated by Igbos, initially of the Onitsha bloc, who were later superseded by the Owerri bloc[45] as noted by Chinua Achebe.

The first group of people from Iduma to move to Port Harcourt did so in late September 1968, as soon as the news of its liberation spread to the villages. The number quickly increased in subsequent years.

The most important reason for the Iduma Port Harcourt drift was the quest for paid employment which could not be secured in the villages. Others, however, came to the city to trade. Yet again, there were those who came to Port Harcourt merely to have a taste of the city life they had long been hearing so much of. However, it is important to note that this last category of persons constituted only a minority. Basically what motivated th

---

[45] Chinua Achebe, op. cit.

e rural-urban drift was not the quest for high-life, but the new status of Port Harcourt, became a way out of the frustrations and sufferings created by the war. In the post-war period, Port Harcourt also made much impact on Idema in the educational realm. The city had been the host of institutions of higher learning such as St John's Teacher Training College, and lately, College of Education and College of Science and Technology (now Rivers State University of Science and Technology). This consequently led to another exodus to Port Harcourt in the late 70s in search of the educational 'golden fleece'. The effects of the war on the community's political system were not as far-reaching as its effects on the economy and the social realms. Nonetheless, there were one or two significant developments during the period.

Following the occupation of Iduma by the federal troops, a committee of para-military officials called "Civil Defence" was established. Existing side by side with this committee was the Boys Scout Movement. These two bodies replaced the pre-war village councilors and performed varied functions. They were generally concerned with the maintenance of Law and order and undertook a supervisory role in the maintenance of sanitation. In addition, they liaised with the king and house heads before decisions on certain matters were taken and effected.

In conclusion, the obvious effects of the Nigerian Civil War on Iduma included disruption of normal political social and economic activities, loss of personal effects and lives and general deprivation.

CHAPTER 8

IDUMA SINCE THE CREATION OF

BAYELSA STATE

Though, there are other reasons for the creation of states , it is often rationalized that it is a means of creating greater opportunities for even political, economic, social and cultural development.

The initial demand for a state by the Bayelsa people came under the aegis of Abayelsa State Movement when the defunct Babangida administration revisited the state creation issue in 1991. The proposed Abayelsa state comprised the present Bayelsa State and the old Ahoada Local Government Area. The proposed state was not created due partly to mutual suspicion, opposition and lack of interest on the part of powerful elites on both sides that is, Ahoada Local Government Area on the one hand and the local government areas that presently constitute

Bayelsa State[1].

The appointment of the Sir Mbanefo Committee and its inauguration on December 13, 1995 by General Sani Abacha raised fresh hopes for the creation of states in the country[2]. The people of the area presently known as Bayelsa having failed to achieve their dreams in earlier attempts adopted new strategies: tw o of such strategies were: (1) by limiting their demand to the six Local Government Areas of Brass, Ekeremor, Ogbia, Sagbama, Southern Ijaw and Yenagoa in their memoranda; (2) by being unanimous in their demand for the creation of Bayelsa State in the memoranda presented to both the Sir Mbanefo Committee and the Head of State respectively, by the Bayelsa State Creation Forum.

By a twist of events, the Sir Mbanefo Committee recommended Bayelsa State amongst the States to be

---

1. Kimse A. B. Okoko, and A. Lazarus, in "The Land and People of Bayelsa
State: Central Niger Delta" E. J. Alagoa (ed), 1999, page 255
2. See, M. N. Alkali et al (eds), Nigeria in the Transition Years: 1993–
1999 Presidential Advisory Committee, (1999), page 17

created. This was subsequently approved by the Provisional Ruling Council (PRC). During the independence broadcast of October 1, 1996, General Sani Abacha announced the creation of Bayelsa State along with five (5) other states[3].

Consistent with the view enunciated that creation of states brings about socio-economic development, this chapter seeks to examine the political developments and socio-economic changes in Iduma since the creation of Bayelsa State.

8.1 Political Developments

Political developments and socio-economic changes in I duma in the period will be better understood and appreciated a gainst the background of a retrospective view of the political, ec onomic and physical landscapes of Bayelsa State when it was cr eated, and during its early years.

---

3. States (Creation and Transitional Provisions) Decree No. 36 of
   1996, page 477 at A 481 – A 503, Gazette No. 72, Vol. 83

This was graphically captured by Dr. J. B. Egberike whil e describing the level of underdevelopment of the state in 2001. According to Dr. Egberike, "Any objective chronicler of the peo ple and events in Bayelsa State since its creation in October 1996 and since the inception of the Alamieyeseigha administration i n May 1999, would recall the floundering state of the economy, the high level of underdevelopment, the low morale of the peop le due to political marginalization and economic deprivation, th e isolation of the state from the rest of the federation due to lack of federal roads linking this littoral state to the hinterland, the a bsence of National Electric Power Authoruty (NEPA) national g rid, the relentless depletion of the natural resources of the peopl e, the restless wheel of economic exploitation grinding and crus hing the Bayelsa people and landscape by the multi-national oil companies, and the insensibility of previous national governments to the physical plight of the Niger Delta, consequent upon the environmental degradation and displacement of the

people from their homesteads and occupation[4].

At creation the young state was faced with these myriads of challenges from all fronts. Though the state was created on October 1, 1996, it was not until October 7, 1996 that Capt. (NN) Oladipo Philip Ayeni was appointed as the Military Administrator for the state.

On assumption of duty, the Military Administrator had to contend with the problems of starting a state which capital city Yenagoa was like a virgin land bereft of any basic infrastructure. The gory state of Yenagoa, was a replicate, if not worse than what the average town in Bayelsa was like at the time.

From a political point of view, Bayelsa could be likened to the distant echoes of a lonely weather-beaten hero of an abandoned tribe crying from the wilderness, calling for social and political re-integration and economic restoration for his marooned people. It is from this point

4. See Dr. J. B. Egberike Introductory note in DSP Alamieyesei gha
   Landmark Speeches, Nengi Josef Ilagha (ed), 2002, Vol. 2, page xiv

of view of a politically marginalized and economically deprived people that we can mirror the state of political developments in Iduma, a principal community in Bayelsa State.

Political developments in Iduma had been slow, as there were very little changes in the early years of Bayelsa State. Going by the Transition to to Civil Rule Programme of events released by the General Sani Abacha-led Military Government; the last quarter of 1996 was for elections into Local Government Councils on party basis. It must be noted that earlier elections had been conducted into the various councils based on zero party platform in Rivers State before the state was created. In that election, Dr. J. I. Ogbomade roundly defeated Mr. Mitema Obodor who contested with him, and emerged as the councillor for Ogbia Ward 1. The election of Dr. Johnson I. Ogbomade into the Ogbia Local Government Council in 1996 raised the morale of most Iduma, giving indication of greater political leverage in the years ahead.

At the end of the tenure of Dr. Ogbomade in the council, pending the conduct of elections under political party platform s, sole administrators, and management committee members were appointed to take care of the various local government councils in the state at the 2nd quarter of 1998. This led to the appointment of Mr. Obegha J. Oworibo as Sole Administrator of Ogbia Local Government Area alondside with four other members namely Chief N. D. Digha, Mr. Branzuk Ikuli, Mrs. Lady Isete and Mr. Emmanuel I. Ogidi. The appointment of Mr. Emmanuel I. Ogidi (now Chief Emmanuel Ogidi-Ene) from the Iduma axis as one of the members by the state government to represent Iduma in the Ogbia Local Government Council was applauded. A development which further enhanced the rising profile of political recognition of Iduma after its exit from the Nembe District of former Brass Local Government Area.

As a means of strengthening community/clan leadership the Bayelsa State Government set out to recognize and classify some Traditional chieftaincy stools in the state. In doing so it set up a Chieftaincy Review and Classification Committee under Sir Gabriel Okara, a reverered poet, writer, and elder statesman. The outcome of that committee was the official recognition of two chieftaincy stools in Abureni clan, being the Olilaema of Idema, and the Olila-Ebhugh Abureni respectively. These stools which the Rivers State Government did not accord recognition after several efforts were eventually recognized. They were accord ingly classified by the Bayelsa State Government and gazetted in March 1999[5].

Following the sudden death of General Sani Abacha on the 8th of June 1998, and the appointment of Major General Abdulsalami Alhaji Abudakar as Head of State of the Federal Military Government, there was increased political activity due to the desire of the military to disengage from governance.

When the lid on political activities was finally lifted in line with the regime's revised Transition to Civil Rule Programme, Iduma sons and daughters also took

---

5. See White paper on the report on the Committee on the recognition and classification of Chieftancy stools in Bayelsa State under the chairmanship of Dr. Gabrial Okara, (1999), pages 1 – 8

advantage by registering themselves with political parties, where they participated actively in the process. A notable political activist from the area such as Madam Evelyn Orukari of blessed memory also contested the primary elections under the PDP platform as an aspirant into the Bayelsa State House of Assembly.

Though, she was not lucky to have emerged as the candidate of choice for her party, her roles were recognized when her party won the governorship election and cleared most of the se ats at the state legislature during the 1999 general elections. She was appointed a member of the Ogbia Rural Development Centre, created by the Alamieyeseigha administration. It must be noted however, that apart from her appointment which was not commensurate with her role in the party, no other Iduma indigene got any appointment elsewhere.

During the period, it was of common knowledge that a new political culture had gained ground not only in Iduma but the entire state. The politics of character assassination and violence which were hitherto unknown in our political history.

The poor state of the Bayelsa State economy arising from the inability of young graduates and school leavers to secure gainful employment, coupled with the despoliation of the environment by multi-national oil companies produced a cabal amongst youths who had become vulnerable to political gladiators and contenders to political offices.

This was the scenario that the traditional leadership in Idema and Obeduma were to contend with during the year 2000 – 2003. It was a trying moment for traditional leadership in the community.

In a letter dated 15, January 2000, HRH F. E. A. Igoniwari, JP, the Olilaema of Idema, was accused to have committed so me impeachable offences[6]. He was served with notice to appear before the villagers at the Idema Community Hall to defend himself of the allegations on Saturday 5th February, 2000. On the appointed date, HRH F. E. A. Igoniwari did not turn up; reasons were not given for his failure. Hence, the Idema community decided to sanction him to keep clear from community matters until such a time he was ready to show cause.

The Ebo family which responsibility was to produce a regent in such circumstance was directed to do so. Consequently, Mr. Justice Joel Edumologbo was presented and held sway as regent for a couple of years before he was removed on 28th November 2009 on grounds of misconduct. He was in the same year replaced by Chief John I. E. Adiboko who acted in that capacity until he died in 2011.

There are recent indications at resolving the differences between HRH F. E. A. Igoniwari, JP, the suspended Olilaema with the Idema Community. The suspended Olilaema had since 2

---

[6] See letter dated 15th January, 2000, and Press Release dated 7th February, 2000, signed on behalf of the Idema Community as Notice and Suspension Order respectively.

013 made representation through members of the Obodiri House to the community. The Olilaema had complied with some of the conditions imposed on him. Reconciliation efforts having reached an advanced stage with the aggrieved persons in the community, and there are positive signs he may be reinstated in the month of March 2017, to coincide with the eyal-odudul festival.

Similarly, in Obeduma Community, the year 2003, turned out to be a very trying time for HRH S. M. A. Opuso, who was allegedly accused of witchcraft. As a result, in July 2003 the Obeduma Community sanctioned him, and demanded that except he cleared himself of the allegations, otherwise, he would cease to be their leader and has since been on suspension. Consequently, Chief Remember Ode, from the Opuso axis of the community was appointed as regent of the community.

Chief Ode's regency was abruptly terminated in 2011 as a result of his refusal to pay a fine imposed on him by the community occasioned by wrong-doing. He assaulted one Mr. Solomon Robert Offor by inflicting him with a deep matchet cut sometime in 2011. It was unbecoming of a regent to behave in such a barbaric manner, and the community imposed a fine on him. It was his refusal to obey the community sanction that led to the temporary transfer of the mantle of leadership from him to Chief Edward S. Awo in his capacity as Chairman, Obeduma C ouncil of Chiefs. Chief E. S. Awo has been acting in that capacity since 2011.

There is recent information that the matter between the suspended Olilaema of Obeduma HRH S. M. A. Opuso and the Obeduma Community is being looked into. The matter is said to have reached its final resolution stage and going by the assurances of the Obeduma Community, HRH S.M.A. Opuso is billed to be reinstated in the month of March 2017.

The year 2008, and 2013 were very eventful in the annals of the political history of Iduma. Firstly, 12th July 2008 witnessed the formal election and installation of an Iduma son, Chief (Barr.) Collins E. Daniel as the first Olila-Ebhugh of Abureni Kingdom and his subsequent presentation to the Chairman of the Bayelsa State Council of Traditional Rulers on 22nd July, 2008.

Similarly, the year 2013 also witnessed the election/installation of Mr. Inatimi Victor Okiori from the Ologo family as the Olilaema of Eboh Community, and Mr. Wilberforce Lele (aka Osimini) from the Ivi family as Deputy Olilaema. Their election/installation put to an end the long period of interregnum or regency in Eboh community, since the demise of HRH Godspower E. Eboh, JP, the last holder of the office in 2007. HRH Inatimi Victor Okiori Eboh and his deputy have since been presented to the Olila-Ebhugh Abureni in Council for recognition, and have been duly recognized.

Although in earlier years, Iduma indigenes were not appointed into political office at the state level, from 2007, this trend changed. A few indigenes of the Community had been appointed into state government agencies as members of commissions and boards.

At the federal level, an indigene, Dr. Temple Offor was appointed as one of the aides to the wife of Former President GoodLuck E. Jonathan, holding the portfolio of Senior Special Assistant (SSA), Domestics. An appointment that could be likened to a Greek gift. This is because through high-wired political intrigues within the presidency, the vibrant, brilliant appointee was eased out within three months of his appointment; he was immediately replaced with one Mr. Waripamowei Dudafa from the Opokuma axis of Bayelsa State.

Indigenes of Iduma have not been elected into any State or federal legislative assembly, despite several failed attempts. Similarly, no indigene of Iduma have been lucky to have been considered suitable for appointment into any judicial office since the death of Magistrate Basoene Joel in 2003.

That notwithstanding, a few brilliant and industrious Iduma indigenes have held high offices at the executive arm in th e public service of Bayelsa State since its creation. For instance, the author held the office of Principal Secretary (Chief of Staff), Government House, during the early years of the state, and also held the position of Permanent Secretary before he retired from the Civil Service. There are also others who got appointed as permanent secretaries, directors in the State Civil Service and as Heads of Departments in the Local Government Service, as well as members of commissions and boards. Over the years Iduma came to be noticed as a Community with a high number of personnel in both the State and Local Government Systems.

The political developments in Iduma since the creation of Bayelsa State though slow in view of the several odds against it, but when compared to the period prior to the inception of Bayelsa State it can be assessed to be progressive.

8.2 Socio – Economic Changes

Since the creation of Bayelsa State Iduma like most other communities in the Niger Delta, have witnessed socio-economic changes. The geo-physical configurations in the Niger Delta have been partly, if not largely responsible for most of these changes.

Elements of ecological degradation and perennial pollution as well as their deleterious effects on the quality of people's li ves generally were hitherto unknown until recent times. The degradation of the environment by the activities of the multi-national oil prospecting companies has led to depletion of local resources.

The traditional occupations of Iduma which includes fishing, farming, canoe carving, palm oil and kernel production, logging, raffia products, etc. being her economic mainstay, have become inadequate to maintain the population, and the new forms of education have become increasingly inadequate to prepare the youth for dignified labour and self- employment.

As multi-national companies and corporations became more actively involved in the exploration and exploitation of crude oil and gas, clashes between them and the youth increased. Issues of pollution, erosion, as well as ecological degradation called for adequate compensation. These youth bore the brunt of unemployment and underemployment.

The youth are taking centre stage in these times, to the consternation of their elders, and they are adopting forms of struggle that are yet to be fully tested and organizational struggles that are somewhat alien in the society.

The authority of the traditional institution of chieftaincy has waned and the much-deserved respect to elders has receeded into the shadows through the operations of party politics and the new elites that have emerged. Societal values have eroded and the temptation of the get rich quick mentality has driven the youth into all sorts of activity including abduction of oil ompany workers. In the most recent times this trend has been extended to fellow citizens, especially persons of affluence in the society. The list of recent unprecedented happenings can go on and on.

Professor E. J. Alagoa, an eminent scholar in his own right, had reminded us a couple of years ago in a public lecture delivered on "The Ijaw Nation in the New Millennium" at the 4th Convention of the Ijaw National Congress at Yenagoa, that "apart from political marginalization, the major problems of the Niger Delta are traceable to economic deprivation" [7]. He illlustrated, by submitting that Niger Delta Youth are "restive" because they are unemployed, hungry and therefore angry. He summed up by saying they are angry, because the vast sums of money realized from the sale of petroleum and gas derived from the Niger Delta are siphoned to other places.

I consider the erudite professor's analysis of the problem from the economic point of view germane having regard to the fact that the economy is the base from which the super structure stands; therefore he cannot be faulted. But closely following this is the factor relating to political indiscipline, with respect to lack of will on the part of the political leadership, due to inability to judiciously put into use the revenue earned from the federation account. In so doing, jobs would have been created and infrastructure built to take care of the rural urban drift.

It is unfortunate that those leaving the rural areas to

---

7. E. J. Alagoa, The Ijaw in the New Millennium, (1999), pages 16 and 17

seek for jobs at the urban centres cannot find employment because the jobs are non-existent.

Perhaps, yet one more reason for the restiveness among the youth of Iduma is the insincerity on the part of the oil prospecting companies in the area, and neglect by the federal government. Iduma has often adopted the internationally accepted principle of asking the polluter to pay for pollution. They also urged the various multinational companies to play a major role, in the development of their communities as compensation for massive pollution suffered by them.

At the same time, the companies would make promises but will not fulfill, and at other times they have argued that the responsibility of developing the communities lay entirely with the federal government to which they regularly paid royalties, r ent and other impositions as and when due. The federal government, itself instead of finding a solution to this matter, engaged in the familiar tactic of passing the buck. Two instances of this problem have played out in Iduma during this period, which I need to mention briefly.

The first was when the Soku gas plant was to be built, Iduma as a stakeholder approached the Shell Petroleum Development Company Limited, and complained bitterly about the pollution and the general degradation of the environment and asked for compensation. No compensation was paid, but rather, it referred the community to the federal government to whom it pays royalty to.

In the early 1990s, when Iduma collaborated with other Ogbia communities and formed a pressure group called Movement For Reparation to Ogbia (MORETO) and presented a charter of demands to the Shell Petroleum Development Company Limited (SPDC), Nigeria Agip Oil Company (NAOC), etc, for crude oil exploration and exploitation activities in Ogbia land since 1956, the same reasons were given and nothing came by way of

reparation to Iduma and the rest of Ogbia[8].

On January 22nd 1998, in the course of the initial development plans of the Santa Barbara Oil Field in one of the stakeholders meetings at Idema, the Iduma Community had presented to the Shell Petroleum Development Company Limited, a number of demands including the building of a skill acquisition centre at Obeduma, and the construction of a road to link Obeduma, Idema and Eboh communities through the old oil well 1 Location Road to Ogbia town[9]. In its response, SPDC through Engr. H. Isi Odiase (SPDC – East, Project Engineer, Santa Barbara projects. In his words "in line with our new policy of sustainable development I am pleased to announce the approval of a construction of a road to link Obeduma-Iduma and Eboh to Ogbia Town in our 1998 programme. Construction will start in 1998. We

---

8. See charter of demands by the Ogbia people of 1/11/92.
9. An address presented by Capt. G. E. Koru rtd., on behalf of the Idema
  community to SPDC, 22/1/98

believe that such a road will open up the communities and attract investors"[10].

Unfortunately, like I have earlier said, this ended

on paper no more no less. Although, after a while, Iduma also keyed into another road project – Otuegila Idema – Nembe Road, expected to be built by SPDC/NDDC.

The attitude of the multi-national oil companies with respect to giving excuses as a means of absolving themselves from liabilities on matters concerning community development is not a new tactic as it has always played out. A case in point is the 42km Otuegila-Idema-Nembe Road Project which SPDC abandoned. All pre-construction activities including surveys, revocation of Rights of Occupancy, etc, was completed for the said road since 2000, and actual construction works were billed to have commenced in January 2002, with a December 2005 as completion date but SPDC suddenly developed cold feet on the road project.

---

10. Address presented by Engr. H.Isi Odiase on behalf of SPDC to Idema,
Eboh and Obeduma communities, Idema on 22/1/98
The road if constructed, would have benefited Iduma and 13 other communities namely: Otuegila, Amorokeni, Amoroto, Emago-Kugbo, Akani, Oluasiri, Okoroba, Agrisaba, Biokponga, Biantubu, Otatubu, Bassambiri, Ogbolomabiri (Nembe).

Sensing that SPDC was up to another game of deceit and intrigues, the would-be beneficiaries of the proposed road project constituted themselves into a pressure group – Otuegila-Idema-Nembe Road Project Forum on 4th November, 2004. Through the activities of the group which include: meetings, rallies, and a world press conference which it organized on May 27, 2005, intended to press home the demand for the construction of the road which had suffered unusual delay.

During the world press conference, the chairman of the group Chief (Barr.) D.K. Derri drew SPDC, and the other development partners' attention on the need to build the road. He also re-emphasized the issue of neglect and deceit on the part of most oil companies, when he said thus: "It is with a deep sense of disappointment, neglect, frustration and pain that we the people (Kings, Chiefs, Elders, Women, Youth, Professionals and elected representatives) of Otuegila, Amorokeni, Amoroto, Emago-Kugbo, Akani, Oluasiri, Iduma, Okoroba, Agrisaba, Biokponga and Nembe – Bassambiri Communities in Ogbia Local Government Area of Bayelsa State, and Abua/Odual Local Government Area of Rivers State have called the world Press Conference to bring to the attention of government, all Nigerians and all people of conscience in the world, of the intolerable plight and continuous deceit to which our various major oil-producing communities have been subjected by the Shell Petroleum Development Company of Nigeria Ltd ("Shell Petroleum") with respect to the unfulfilled Otuegila-Idema-Nembe Road Project besides a litany of other countless unfulfilled promises"[11]

---

11. Press Statement/Address presented by Chief Danfebo K. Derri
 on behalf of the Otuegila – Idema – Nembe Road Project Forum
 at the World Press Conference held in Otuegila, Ogbia on May
 27, 2005.

However, the prospects for the construction of this very important road was later consumed by the twin factors of intrigues and deceit by the oil companies especially SPDC, and the unnecessary Bassambiri and Ogbolomabiri (Nembe) rivalry on the issue of routing of the said road.

The Ogbolomabiri section of Nembe preferred that the road passed through Opume, Akipelai, Etiema to Nembe, while the Bassambiri section of Nembe insisted that the original route of the road as designed to benefit fourteen (14) communities through the – Otuegila axis via Idema – Nembe should be maintained.

In the ensuing disagreements, the two principal bodies namely – Nembe Ibe Road Project Group and Otuegila–Idema–Nembe Road Project Forum were invted to a meeting with the stakeholders at Government House, Yenagoa, for purposes of harmonizing the groups' positions.

The said meeting which was presided over by Dr. Goodluck E. Jonathan, Deputy Governor of Bayelsa State (as he then was) on behalf of the Governor, it was resolved that the two road projects should be executed by the NDDC/SPDC simultaneously for the interest of the affected communities. Unfortunately, over a decade since that agreement was reached between the various stakeholders in the presence of the Bayelsa State Government, there has not been any effort by either the SPDC or NDDC to do any work on the Otuegila – Idema – Nembe Road Project.

After some horse-trading by the political bigwigs in Nembe Kingdom and other interest groups within the Bayelsa State Government, the NDDC/SPDC finally commenced work on the route preferred by the Ogbolomabiri section of Nembe, using the shorter distance and the overall project cost as excuses.

It is important to note that the road has been over politicized and it has still not been completed by the contractor – SETRACO NIGERIA LTD. The question one is tempted to ask is that; has any of the multi-national companies who are in a joint vent ure arrangement with the federal government given any excuse (s) not to exploit crude oil from the area? Or has the NNPC stopped the sale of oil exploited from the area the road is proposed to be built?

The answer will be in the negative because both are only interested on what they will get from the area. This, in my mind is social injustice, and it boils down to leadership failure. Hence the renowed author Chinua Achebe once said that the trouble with Nigeria is simply and squarely a failure of leadership[12].

The prospects of this project was consumed partly by the unwillingness and insincerity on the part of Shell Petroleum Development Company (SPDC) to develop Iduma, and the unhealthy rivalry for supremacy between Ogbolomabiri and Bassambiri – the two principal towns of the Nembe Kingdom. The Otuegila-Idema-Nembe Road Project if constructed would have opened up that axis of the State to development.

---

12. Chinua Achebe, The Trouble with Nigeria, (1983), page 1

In later years the multi-national companies, operating in Iduma and other parts of the Niger Delta, had reviewed their approach on the execution of development projects to communities, by adopting the General Memorandum of Understanding (GMOU) model for development project. By this method, comm unities were grouped into clusters, and City Trusts, and capital funds pooled into a Cluster Board to be shared among the various City Trusts within the cluster. This brought into being the Abureni Cluster Development Board through which fund was appropriated to Iduma City and Obeduma City Trust respectively, to enable them execute priority projects from the fund allocated to their City Trust.

The Shell Petroleum Development Company (SPDC) had through this method, executed the following projects in Iduma.

(i)   Iduma Town Hall
(ii)   Iyoaburu foot-bridge
(iii)   Iduma - Idema link foot-bridge
(iv)   Electrification of Obeduma community, including the purchase and installation of a 60KVA generating set.

Economic activities in Iduma would only be enhanced if the community is opened up by motorable roads. The federal and the state governments appear not concerned about the plight of its citizenry. The social and economic changes taking place in the community whereby most youth have abandoned the tr aditional occupation and are attracted to party politics, and are merely errand boys to political bigwigs in the state as well as their involvement in activities inimical to the environment such as bunkering and other activities is certainly not a good development for societal growth. This phenomenon was brought about by the activities of multi-national companies whose activities have led to pollution and general environmental degradation. These oil companies have cared little about the general well-being of the people in their areas of operation.

8.3 Iduma in Ogbia Brotherhood

The Ogbia Brotherhood is a socio-cultural organization founded in October, 1940 at Oloibiri by the Ogbia people through the initiative of Rev. George Igabu Amangala.

The motto of the Ogbia Brotherhood as captured in its Constitution is "All for Each and Each for All"[13]. Both the preamble to the Constitution and the motto reinforces the aim of the organization as being principally to create a common identity and forge unity and progress amongst the Ogbia people.

Though founded since October 1940, the Iduma people could not play an active role in the organization because it was dislocated from the rest of Ogbia, since it was administered under the Nembe District for almost a Century.

Iduma sons and daughters that were in the Ogbia Brotherhood at the time can best be described as being

---

13. Ogbia Brotherhood Constitution (as amended) 2008, pages 1 - 36

there by association but not as active members. One of the few Iduma indigenes who fell into this category was Mr. John Koru of blessed memory. His early career in the Civil Service in Oloibiri may have also facilitated his close association with the Ogbia Brotherhood.

Iduma activities in the Ogbia Brotherhood began to be noticed during the electioneering campaigns of Chief Melford Okilo as governorship candidate of the National Party of Nigeria (NPN), and when he eventually won the general elections in 1979 as the first Civilian Governor of Rivers State. When Iduma and most of the Abureni Communities were first transferred to Ogbia District from its hitherto Nembe District, Iduma's involvement in Ogbia Brotherhood matters and activities was accelerated. The Ogbia people have always taken Iduma as their brothers in spite of the fact that they were being administered under Nembe District for administrative convenience.

Iduma interest in Ogbia Brotherhood matters was further activated when on 25th November, 1991 she broke loose from

215

Nembe hegemony and join her kith and kin in the newly created Ogbia Local Government Council. In order to assure the Iduma people that they were in safe hands, Mr. Eric Aworabhi, the Sole Administrator of Ogbia Local Government Council (as he then was) arranged a familiarization tour to Iduma within three weeks of his appointment.

The creation of Bayelsa State in 1996 gave further impetus to the undoubting active participation of Iduma indigenes in Ogbia Brotherhood matters. In order to properly integrate the Iduma and the rest of Abureni into the Ogbia Brotherhood, constitution amendment exercises were carried out in 2008 and 2011 for both the Ogbia Brotherhood Constitution and that of the Obanobhan respectively. During that exercise Iduma and the rest of Abureni were thus properly reflected in the said constitution as an autonomous clan within the Ogbia ethnic nationality[14].

---

14. Obanobhan Ogbia Constitution, 2011 as amended, pages 1 - 20

CHAPTER 9

EXTERNAL RELATIONS WITH NEIGHBOURS

The Iduma people did not live in isolation with its neighbours. Iduma had existed along with several neighbours, immediate and more distant, including also its Abureni neighbours. These relations have had their ups and downs. This chapter seeks to examine these relations over time.

9.1　Iduma and Her Abureni Neighbours

The Iduma people saw themselves as belonging to a wider group called Abureni comprising Iduma, Obo-Agboin (Kugbo), Edumanom (Okoroba). The Okoroba people call themselves Okorobo, while they are known within Abureni as Edumanom, though their Ogbia immediate neighbours prefer calling them Emeke. Over the years, the name Okoroba is generally being used and thus giving vent to the possibility that Okoroba may be a corruption of Okorobo. I had listed the composite communities of these sub-groups in earlier chapters; doing so again shall amount to repetition, which may not add any value.

These communities speak the same language [1]. They also share many items of culture and depended on their livelihood on similar combinations of farming and fishing. Though, some writers tend to classify these communities into two sub language clusters and at other times language sub-groups of Kugbo and Abureni. I submit that any such language classification is obvio usly dubious, lacking in substance and proper study of Abureni forms and may have been politically motivated.

The Abureni language is unique and distinct and is spoken by all the Abureni communities and understood by all the Abureni communities. The fact that there are slight dialectical differences cannot be seen as sufficient reason for a further division of the language.

---

1. E. E. Efere and Kay Williamson, "Langaugaes" in E. J. Alagoa(ed) The Land and People of Bayelsa State, Central Niger Delta, Port Harcourt, 1999, page 97, and 104, And coroboration from personal interview with Elder Ediaman Jackson, circa 86 years. Emago-Kugbo, 25/10/83

The Iduma people believe that problems arising from land disputes and other related matters could be resolved amongst themselves. Hence, from time to time the village heads of these communities converge at chosen places to hear and resolve cases between the villages. These villages from time to time also organize wrestling contests amongst themselves as a way of promoting unity within the clan. In present times, the game of football has gained so much fame and publicity-football tournaments are also being organized amongst the villages from time to time.

A festival known as Eyal-Ilobhiri to the Iduma in particular and Eyal-Ikai to Opume, Akipelai, Okoroba and eyal odudul to the generality of all Abureni is common amongst them. The eyal odudul is an eight-day festival celebrated by all the major Abureni villages including Opume and Akipelai as a mark of their common culture.

The festival marked the end of the farming season and is held annually in March. The commencement date for the festival is dictated by the tide and the movement of the moon. The tidal water which has its ebb and full tide, and the movement of the moon are very significant determinants in the timing of the festival. It is a lunar rather than numerical month that most African societies including Abureni use in the recording of calendar of events, because events of the moon change.

Some special features of the festival include the performance of certain rites and the staging of the popular Akara masquerade also known as Ekelekpum. The Akara masquerade display is the climax of the festival. The festival offered both the young and old the opportunity of watching the Akara masquerade dance.

The common belief held by the Abureni clan was that sanctions of the gods and the will of man determine good yields. This belief also holds sway in most African societies[2].

The period was an epoch-making occasion in Iduma when it was being observed. Sacrifices and

---

2. John S. Mbitu, African Religions and philosophy, London, (1969), page 41

libations were poured to the different deities and holy shrines in the land: Iyobio, Obo-Awuruma, Ibe, Igbiani, Abedi-Eboh, Oguofurugu, Onem, Alukpesi, Enai-Ema[3], etc.

Iduma relations with her Abureni neighbours had been relatively cordial over the years. They have assisted one another in times of great distress and need. For instance, Okoroba readily came to the aid of Iduma and played host to some of its indigenes during the Nigerian Civil War, when Iduma was sacked by the Biafran forces. In 1992, during the Nembe and Iduma misunderstandings arising from the dispute over Ijaw-kiri between Kalabari and Nembe, Emago-Kugbo and Akani (Oghan) played host to Iduma indigenes who went into hiding, in the wake of Nembe hostilities.

In spite of this cordial relationship, there were periods this relationship came under severe stress and strain. Though expectedly, as humans, misunderstandings

---

3. Joe E. Ogidi, circa 65 years, Idema, 25/08/84

are bound to arise but the ability to contain them is the hallmark of maturity. For instance, in the 1940s, the disputed Iyobia land matter between the Apere family of Okoroba and Idema brought serious misunderstanding and strained the relationship between Iduma and Okoroba. Again, the role played by three indigenes of Emago-Kugbo that led to the sacking of Iduma in May, 16th 1968, during the Nigerian Civil War also brought about strained relations between Iduma and Emago-Kugbo.

These strained relations were overcome over the years by Iduma and her Abureni neighbours, through marital relationships, inter-personal contacts and the overall realization of the need for the peace and unity of all Abureni at home and in diaspora.

This ideal was further cemented by the establishment of the Abureni Forum in Port Harcourt by indigenes of Abureni Communities resident in Port Harcourt at the end of the Civil War. Through the forum, inter-community matters were resolved, clan based burial meetings were held, and it has since remain an organ of Abureni for the promotion of peace and unity and the welfare of all Aburenis.

Abureni elites through collaborative effort, since the creation of Bayelsa State formed "Abureni Onin", a socio-cultural organization aimed at fostering unity, peaceful co-existence and attracting development to all Abureni Communities in Rivers and Bayelsa States. "Abureni Onin" had through its activities promoted peaceful co-existence and ensured the prevalence of law and order in Abureni communities, including good neighbourliness.

Similarly, a Christian outreach – Abureni Evangelical Outreach, had not only promoted Christianity amongst Abureni communities, but has been in the fore-front of organizing crusades and other peace-related programmes, including medi-care, etc, which has helped a great deal in promoting unity and peaceful co-existence and generally healthy relations in Abureni.

Iduma indigenes have been playing very critical roles in all these organizations, including serving as arbiters in the settlement of intra and inter-community disputes and misunderstandings. On the whole, Iduma relations with her Abureni immediate neighbours have been cordial as marriages and burial ceremonies are still being very participatory, giving full indications that all is well.

9.2. External Relations with other Neighbours

The Iduma people did not live in isolation from their other neighbours. Iduma's other neighbours include: Nembe (Adebe), Kalabari (Akalabari), Odual (Oduan), Odioma, and Otuab agi. Iduma have had relations with some of her neighbours spanning hundreds of years.

These relations have been characterized with a good measure of relative cordiality, and at the same time a measure of tension. This is because both oral and available written sources indicate both friendly and unfriendly relations with these neighbours.

I will like to examine these relations in time perspectives taking each community in sequence.

9.2 (i)   Relations with Nembe (Adebe)

Iduma relations with Nembe (Adebe), spanned through hundreds of years. The relations between Iduma and Nembe (Adebe) at early times was said to be stable, and cordial until the pre-colonial times, at the peak of the slave trade era, when it was characterized with tension, and in later years by domination before Iduma broke loose from Nembe political hegemony. However, there were also periods when the relations were fairly cordial. Thus they talk on the one hand of trade, and on the other hand of piracy, raids and head hunting. Nembe continues to echo in Iduma oral tradition as a neighbour whose pervasive slave raids on its communities provoked wars which periodically engulfed both communities[4].

4. E. J. Alagoa, The Small Brave City State, 1964, page 60

As we saw earlier, it was the persistent Nembe raids on Iduma that compelled King Igoniwari the (1st) of Iduma to relocate his community to a more strategic site across the bank of the river to face such challenges.

The Iduma people, being far from docile, put up heavy resistance against Nembe attacks. In certain cases indeed they won notable victories and humiliated the enemy. This tradition tells how a certain King Mein of Bassambiri – Nembe was routed in one of these raids in a manner that shamed the whole of Nembe. Again in another instance, it was reported how Iduma organized a punitive expedition to capture this very King Mein alive but did not succeed and in the alternative captured his wife at home[5]. The Nembe version on the other hand claimed that King Mein's wife was rather secretly killed by the Iduma people in a manner that provoked

---

5. Informants were:
   1. Chief Isu Oga, circa 102 years, Idema, 17/08/84,

2. Elder Edward Wills, circa 71 years, Bassambiri – Nembe, 20/3/85.

Bassambiri - Nembe. Consequently, war ensued between both communities[6]. Iduma indeed took pride in its war-like activities. Hence its drum praise.

"Obo Iduma gbori bio gbori bio
Obo Iduma gbori bio gbori bio
Toru paka ikio fa"

Meaning: "Great Iduma of one mind
Great Iduma of one mind
Once out in the river knows no friend"

There was also a good measure of cordiality in Iduma – Nembe relations on account of trade. Economic relations constitute the core of the ties between Iduma and Nembe, since Iduma and the rest Abureni communities had been one of the main supply lines for Nembe foodstuff and other forest products.

Economic relations between Iduma and Nembe have evolved over the centuries, and by the 18th and 20th

---

6. Chiefs Dick Harry Braide and Ors V Chiefs Egbelu and Allagoa and Ors Op. Cit.

centuries, it was said Iduma and the other Abureni agricultural produce accounted for the bulk of the trade with Nembe. These include cash crops like Palm produce, timber, canoes, etc. Iduma bought a range of articles such as gun powder as well as Dane guns, twine, cutlasses and matchets, beads, spirits and rum, salt, seafood, etc. Since the pre-colonial and colonial days, economic relations between Iduma and Nembe had grown.

The beginning of the 20th Century however, marked a new era in the relations between Nembe and Iduma, characterized by domination. The colonial administration introduced a system whereby smaller groups were administered under strong and notable chiefs without minding their various cultural backgrounds. This is how Iduma having guarded her sovereignty came under one administrative authority with other groups such as Nembe, Ogbia and Odual (Oduan). This resulted to several complaints arising from domination and discriminations that were not attended to by the colonial and successive governments.

The other factors that led to poor relations between Iduma and Nembe during the period include:

i. The lack of respect on the rights of the host communities by Nembe settlers;
ii. The seeming support given to settlers by the Nembe

community in the event of any dispute or disagreement between settlers and their host communities;

iii. The failure on the part of Iduma to show restraint on the settlers, whenever provoked or when an act of trespass had been noticed.

The high point of Iduma – Nembe relations was witnessed in 1991. Following the creation of Ogbia Local Government Council from the old Brass Local Government Council Area, Iduma had expressed her desire to be part of the newly created Ogbia Local Government Council, and that request was granted.

The Bassambiri section of Nembe was particularly angered by Iduma's move to join their kith and kin in Ogbia. The step taken by Iduma was seen by the Bassambiri people as a loss to them in their quest for supremacy with the larger and more prominent section of Nembe Community (Ogbolomabiri).

Iduma, Kugbo, and Odual also submitted memoranda as interested parties, and participated in the Justice R. B. Akere Commission of Inquiry set up by the Rivers State Government for boundary-related issues between Brass and Akuku Toru Local Government Areas[7].

This was misunderstood by the Nembe people and interpreted to mean that Iduma had taken sides with the Kalabaris.

These two actions taken by Iduma was considered an affront by the Bassambiri – Nembe Community which led to acts of hostility. In the process, several lives were lost on both sides in the crisis. This resulted to the severance of relations between the two communities for a

---

7. Rivers State of Nigeria – conclusion of the Government of Rivers State on the Report of the Judicial Commission of Enquiry into the disturbanies and conflicts between Akuku –Toru and Brass Local Government Area of Rivers State under the chairmanship of Hon. Justice Peter B. Akere, August, 1993, pages 1 – 16.

period spanning to a decade before relations were normalized in the year 2004.

9.2 (ii) Relationship with Kalabari

Iduma and Kalabari have enjoyed broadly good relations spanning for hundreds of years. Iduma is said to have had its progenitors from the Kalabari Community of 'Ke', a town known for its great antiquity.

Again, following the reprisal attacks on Nembe City as an aftermath of the January 29, 1895 Akassa raid, trading activities on the Brass River had a lull, and the centre of oil trading bus iness shifted to Abonnema. Iduma as a producer community began some serious business relations with the Kalabaris, as a result of the shift.

There are also traditions linking Iduma to raids at the Kalabari communities of Soku and Kula by her war parties in retaliation for hostilities suffered on the hands of these communities, or aggression on the basis of test of might.

Mutual raiding between Iduma and Soku was brought to an end by a covenant which forbade the kidnapping of an Iduma man by a Soku for sacrifice to their national deity and enjoined the protection of Iduma people within Soku territory. On the other hand, the covenant also enjoined Iduma people to respect and protect Soku people within their territory[8].

Iduma relations with Kula Community over time enjoyed relative cordiality. And to ensure a more sustainable relationship, both communities entered into a covenant of mutual protection and that has been sustained over time. Both communities have accorded respect to their defined water boundaries which had often been the sources of disagreements. Kula and Iduma have recognized the need for peaceful co-existence and still give respect to their age-old covenant to date.

Kalabari – Iduma relations reached a sour point

---

8. Mr. Obu Edoghotu circa 71 years, Idema, personal Interview 25/3/78

during the first decade of the 20th Century. This had earlier been stated in the celebrated case of Chiefs Dick Harry Braide and Ors of Degema representing the people of Saka Kugbo and Idema vs Chiefs Egbelu and Allagoa of Brass representing the people of Brass.

In this case the plaintiffs had sought for a declarative judgment that the Iduma people sold themselves for their protection and that they owned Iduma and their properties. Chief Allagoa and Chief Egbelu of Nembe were defendants in the matter. The matter came before His Honour Justice A.F.C. Webber of the Supreme Court of the Protectorates of the Colony of Southern Nigeria at the Calabar Division for hearing and decision on 3rd March, 1913.

To the greatest disappointment of both parties, the court ruled that the Idemas were independent people, and they were entitled to their properties[9]. The plaintiffs were

---

9. See Chief Dick Harry Braide and ors vs Chief Egbelu and Allagoa and ors, Op. Cit.

awarded heavy costs for their misadventure. The judicial pronouncement of Justice Webber saved the Iduma people from the imperialist tendencies of these "local super powers", in their own rights.

Economic relations constitute the core of the ties between Iduma and Kalabari during and after the colonial era. Iduma's agricultural produce accounted for part of the trade with Kalabari. These include: palm produce, and timber, dugout canoes, etc. Iduma bought articles such as Dane guns, cooking utensils, cutlasses, matchets, spirits, jugs, etc. Since the colonial era and after, economic relations between Iduma and Kalabari has grown.

9.2 (iii) Relations with Odual (Oduan)

There are traditions linking Iduma to raids at Adada and Emelego by her war-parties in retaliation suffered. Most of these conflicts were actually resolved by the test of might and thereafter these communities and Iduma entered into blood covenants (ijo) with their opponents. For instance, the raid she organized on Adada and Emelego in the Odual area brought about a covenant between Iduma and Odual which ruled that both communities must henceforth be at peace[10].

One injunction of this covenant forbade the killing of any tsetse fly which perched on either an Oduan or Iduma man[11]. This was arrived at avoiding dropping of blood from either person since the tsetse fly was believed to have sucked the blood of the person it perched on. Since then, Iduma and Oduan relations have improved.

9.2 (iv) Relations with Odioma

Iduma and Odioma relations spanned over hundreds of years. Both communities are said to share common water boundaries at the southern axis, and have had cordial relations ever since. Iduma have maintained

---

10   Informants were:
    i. Mr. Nathaniel Godswill, circa 58 years, Idema, 25/4/87,
    ii. Madam Iseti Amon, circa 74 years, 3/06/82
11   Informants were:
    i. Madam Victoria Offor, circa 65 years, Idema,
    ii. Mr. Ekitei W. Appolo, circa 70 years, 25/08/2010

and respected her age-old boundary line with the Odioma Community, which has been reciprocated. This suggests why both communities have co-existed without any rancour and misunderstanding over the years. There is also no tradition of any blood covenant between Iduma and Odioma.

9.2 (v) Relations with Otuabagi

Iduma maintains a north-west land boundary with Otuabagi and both communities have had cordial relations over the years. There has not been any cause for a blood covenant, and no tradition has mentioned it.

On the whole through these covenants, war-like relations gave way to peace. And in the wake of peace came the trading relations between Iduma and her neighbours which we have already discussed.

CHAPTER 10
SUMMARY AND CONCLUSION

Iduma city in the present Ogbia Local Government Area of Bayelsa State is evidently of great antiquity. The history of her traditions of origin migrations and settlement linking her progenitors to Ke, who were later joined in the settlement by other migrants from the ancient Ebala Kingdom, Odual, and the immediate Ayun-Amorokoin has undoubtedly given her a unique bl end of several cultures including Kalabari-Ijaw, Ogbia and Odual.

From the pre-colonial through the colonial period, the community was able to produce goods to meet her own needs and considerable surpluses for exports. There was a high degree of self-sufficiency of the individual household, and factors making for the concentration of political power in the hands of a minority could not develop. Hence the system of town government was highly democratic, and matters affecting the entire community were most of the time left for the Town Assembly to deliberate upon.

Due to her peculiar position, bounded by two powerful City-States of Nembe and Kalabari, her political, economic and social freedoms were to some extent restricted throughout the nineteenth century. This explains why she was unable to trade directly with the Europeans until colonial times.

Fierce competition ensued between the coastal middlemen and the contending imperial forces represented by the Royal Niger Company. In all cases, Iduma as producers never had a fair deal in the flourishing trade in palm oil and kernel, but served the interest of the coastal middlemen in the first instance, and that of a global trade system represented by the biggest monopolist in the crowd, the Royal Niger Company.

Although the advent of colonial rule led to escape from this economic restriction, the new political system introduced by the colonial authorities in their quest for strong and powerful chiefs through whom to rule small groups in spite of cultural differences for administrative convenience, brought Iduma into Nembe political domination which lasted for decades.

From early colonial times to the Nigerian Civil War, Iduma did not attach much premium on Western education, despite the fact that missionary activities got to Iduma in the last decade of the 19th century. This attitude of unpreparedness to imbibe change was due to her holding on to her age old traditional beliefs and practices.

The Nigeria Civil War brought about changes in the world view of Iduma indigenes, due to the massive rural-urban drift for several reasons. At the end of the war, Iduma youth found education as a veritable tool for social change and development. A lot have since obtained various academic degrees and other qualifications and are favourably competing with youth from other communities.

Iduma over the years has realized the causes of her political marginalization, and has since broken loose from Nembe political domination to join her kith and kin in Ogbia Local Government Area, where they are more acceptable and recognized.

The creation of Bayelsa State since October 1996 has led to some political, economic and social developments in Iduma. However, the activities of multi-national oil companies operating in the area have not helped the community rather it has brought misery occasioned by pollution, and general environmental degradation. This has affected both her economic and social life. The oil prospecting and exploitation companies do not seem to be genuine in their promise to develop the community; so is the federal government also, as both are engaged in a blame game with each other. Hence no meaningful sustainable development project has been embarked upon by either of the two, despite the contribution of the community to national development. The few projects executed are not of priority to the community, and have no bearing on economic emancipation.

The resultant harmful effects of the activities of the multi-national companies have wrecked the environment, and national resources have been depleted. This has given rise to agitation for resource ownership and control, and eventually militancy in Iduma.

The political class has not also helped matters, as priority is given to personal political activities rather than channeling the resources earned from the federation account into sustainable development. How all these would be resolved is a matter of time but greater responsibility lies with the government at all levels.

The Iduma people have never lived in isolation. She has existed along with several neighbours such as Nembe, Kalabari, Odioma and Odual as external neighbours and with Okoroba, Kugbo and Otuabagi as immediate Abureni/Ogbia neighbours. These relations have had their ups and downs.

Economic relations constitute the core of the ties of some of these relations. Due to the hostilities that ensued between Iduma, and some of her neighbours, covenants were made to bring about peace and in the wake of peace came trading relations with Iduma.

In all of these, Iduma has been very resilient.

APPENDIX 1

Family tree of the central delta group

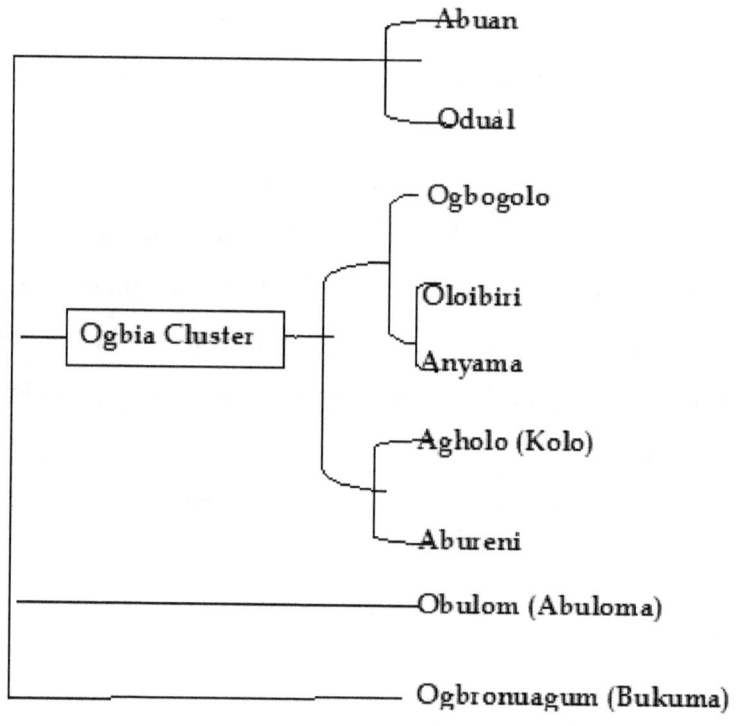

Source: Kay Williamson, 'A Common Language for the Ijaw Ethnic Nationality?' in The Izon of the Niger Delta, (eds) E. J. Alagoa et al, Port Harcourt: Onyoma Research Publications, (2009), p.113 with new in put from the author.

APPENDIX II

KING LIST AND GENEALOGY:

IDUMA

1. OMONGI (OMOYE) — (Founding father/leader of the migrant group from Ke. He was said to have died at Idumanamugbo)

2. FENIBO — (Brother to Omongi and father to Eghunuma, Awo is also claiming paternity.)

3. IDUMA — (Son of Omongi, and Father to Aye, Eboh, and Obe)

4. AYE (IDEMA) — (First Son of Iduma)

Source: i. Chief Isu O. Oga, 102 years, Idema, (12/8/84)

ii. Elder Lionel Joel Edumologbo, 65 + yrs, Idema (11/8/84)

* Iduma that was abandoned in those early years has since the year 2008 been resettled and given a metropolitan city status for all Iduma and the rest of Abureni as the Clan Headquarters.

APPENDIX III

KING LIST AND GENEALOGY OF IDEMA (AYE)

1. IGONIWARI AYE (THE 1ST)

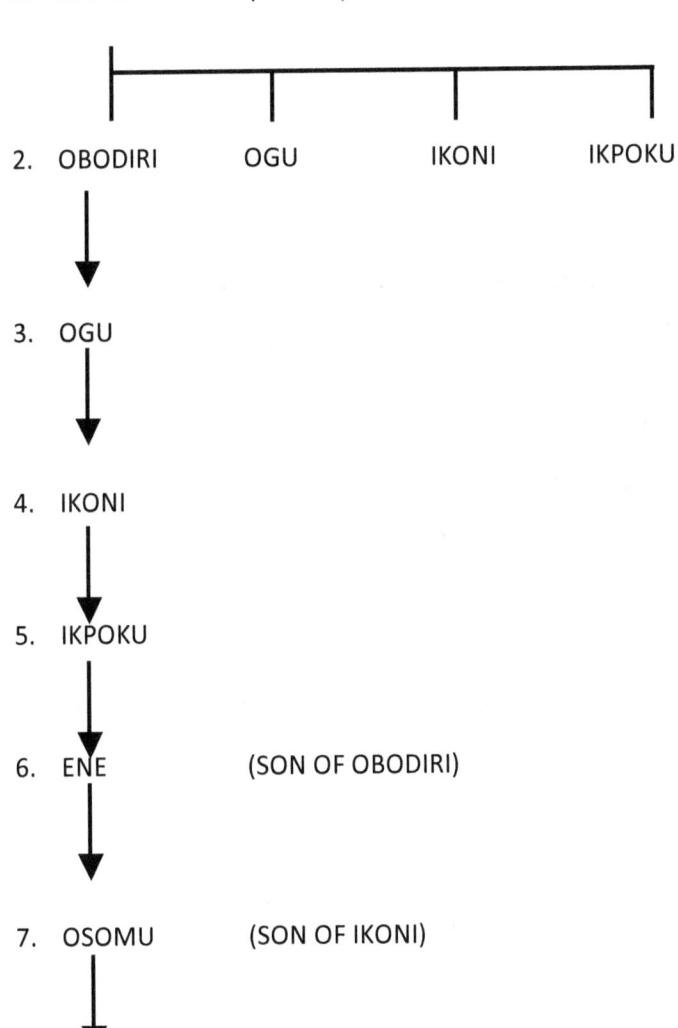

2. OBODIRI   OGU   IKONI   IKPOKU

3. OGU

4. IKONI

5. IKPOKU

6. ENE   (SON OF OBODIRI)

7. OSOMU   (SON OF IKONI)

8. ALOKI   (SON OF OBODIRI)

↓

9. OTOLO   (SON OF IKPOKU

↓

10. IKULI   (d. 1929 – belong to the Obodiri lineage)

↓

11. ABIOSI ADEWARI   (d. 1963 – belong to the Ikoni lineage maternally)

↓

12. FELIX E. ABOKO IGONIWARI the (XII), (a. April 1974 – belong to the Aloki family of the Obodiri lineage maternally)

* Ebutu is also recorded as one of the sons of Igoniwari, but the four recognised royal families are Obodiri, Ogu, Ikoni and Ikpoku from time immemorial.

Source: (i) HRH Felix E. A. Igoniwari the (XII) (JP) 75+ Yrs, Idema 7/4/85
(ii) Mr. Sokari A. Adewari, 65 yrs, Idema 2 5/2/92

APPENDIX IV

KING LIST/TRADITIONAL LEADERS OF EBOH

1. EBOH

2. OLOGO

3. OZIL

4. ATIGHA

5. AKE

6. ADAAFA

7. AKPANA

8. RUFUS

9. GODSPOWER (1984 – 2007

10. VICTOR INATIMI OKIORI (a. 2013)

Source: Victor Inatimi Okiori

APPENDIX V

KING LIST/TRADITIONAL LEADERS OF OBEDUMA

1. OBE

2. OPUSO

3. ABBA

4. IKATA

5. ONBU

6. ODO

7. OGIRI

8. OKEKE

9. IDAH

10. EKERE

11. IPIAN (Regent)

12. SIMEON M. AKE (a. 4th April 1980)

Source: (i) Simeon M. Ake
(ii) Elder Orlu Samuel

APPENDIX VI

A. Primary Sources

i. Oral Evidence: List and Particulars of Informants

S/no.	Name	Status	Address	Age	Date of Interview
1	HRH Felix E. A. Igoniwari, JP	Olilaema of Idema	Idema	75 + yrs	7/4/85
2	John I. E. Adioboko	Chief in Idema	Idema	81 + yrs	25/7/08 & 10/8/11
3	Chief Ngogo Chief in Ke Owitubo		Ke	75 + yrs	8/9/84

4	Mr. S. B. N gogo	Chief in Ke	Ke	72 + yrs	8/9/84
5	Mr. Nwoke D. Agbani	Chief in Ke	Ke	70 + yrs	8/9/84
6	Chief S. O. Benebo	Chief in Ke	Ke	circa 70 + yrs	8/9/84
7	Capt. Glory E. Koru (rtd.)	Elder in Idema	Idema	70 + yrs	27/10/16
8	HRH S.M. A. Opuso	Olilaema of Obeduma	Obeduma	73 + yrs	8/4/85
9	Chief Johnny J. Eghunuma	Chief in Iduma	Iduma	74 + yrs	6/9/84
10	Chief Isu Otolo-Oga	Chief in Idema	Idema	102 + yrs	12/8/84
11	Chief Ibitamuno L. E. – Obodiri	Chief in Idema	Idema	44 + yrs	6/9/84
12	Mr. Orlu Samuel	Elder in Obeduma	Obeduma	72 + yrs	5/4/85
13	Madam Ikokosi Ogumade	Elder in Eboh	Eboh	circa 85 + yrs	10/8/84
14	Mrs. Eliza	Farmer in Id	Idema	circ	21/8/84

	beth O. Daniel	ema		a 45 + yrs	
15	Mr. Ekine Apollo	Palm Oil/Kernels Producer in Idema	Idema	43 + yrs	15/8/84
16	Mr. Sunday Joel	- Do -	Idema	circa 56 + yrs	15/8/84
17	Mr. Akio Johnson	Thatch maker in Idema Idema		circa 65 8/8/84 + yrs	
18	Madam Mammy Johnson	Farmer in Idema	Idema	circa 68 + yrs	6/7/84
19	Madam Victoria Offor	Local Crafts Producer in Idema	Idema	circa 52 + yrs	6/7/94
20	Mr. I. J. Abigo	Asst. Chief Conservator of Forest	Rivers State Min. of Agric. & Nat. Resources P. H.	57 + yrs	4/8/84

21	Mr. Lionel Elder in Idema J. Edumollogbo	Idema		circa 78 + yrs	11/8/84 & 11/8/2005
22	Madam Marian Daniel	Elder in Idema	Idema	circa 60 + yrs	
23	Chief Napoleon Ada	Retired Civil Servant	Abuloma	62 + yrs	14/12/16
24	Mr. Friday Amaegbe	Retired Manager UAC Ltd	Bassambiri	62 + yrs	25/4/2006
25	Mr. Ebimawot Elder in Idemao Daniel		Idema	86 + yrs	21/3/85 & 21/05/2014
26	Dr. Oyetayo	Lecturer	Dept of Zoology, University of Port Harcourt		6/2/85
27	Madam Godspower Johnson	Fisher woman in Idema	Idema	circa 61 yrs	22/8/84
28	Chief George Okoni OduChief i		Idema	circa 98	12/8/78

	n Idema -Eme			yrs	
29	Mr. Sokari A. Adewari	Civil Servant	Idema	circa 65 yrs	25/2/92
30	Mr. Alfred Samuel	Fisherman/ Elder	Obeduma	circa 72 yrs	4/4/85
31	Chief Dakipre Garrick	Chief in Oboghe	Oboghe	63 yrs	5/2/15
32	Daniel Oruan	Founding father of St. John's Anglican Church Idema Idema		circa 101 yrs	25/2/76
33	Mr. Elijah Obinah	Civil Servant	Obeduma	68 yrs	5/9/90
34	Chief Melford O. Okilo	Political leader, Rivers/Bayelsa State	Port Harcourt	68 yrs	20/06/2003
35	Chief Tombibi Ikuli-Ene	Chief in Idema	Idema	circa 60 yrs	4/4/85
36	Elder Ediaman Jackson	Elder in Emago-Kugbo	Emago-Kugbo	circa 86 yrs	25/10/83

37	Mr. Joe Ekere Ogidi	Elder of Sekiapu Society Idema	Idema	circa 65 yrs	25/8/84
38	Mr. Edward Wills	Elder in Bassambiri	Bassambiri, Nembe	circa 71 yrs	20/8/85
39	Mr. Obu Edoghotu	Head of Sekiapu Society, Idema	Idema	circa 71 yrs	25/3/82
40	Mr. Nathaniel Godswill	Industrial worker	Idema	circa 58 yrs	8/9/84
41	Madam Iseti Amon	Farmer/Elder in Idema	Idema	circa 74 yrs	3/6/82
42	Mr. Ekitei Carpenter in Obedumcirca W. Apollo	Obeduma	a	70 yrs	25/8/10
43	Mr. Ayebanoa S. Adewari	Civil Servant	Idema	34 yrs	9/8/84
44	Chief I. L. Ivi	Chief in Eboh	Eboh	76 + yrs	2/08/16

GLOSSARY

ABARAH - Swamp Land

ABURENI - The name of the clan in which Iduma is a part.

ADEBE - The name Nembe is called by the Abureni people

AGHOLO - The traditional name for Kolo Community

AKUBU - axe

AKAIN - Thatch

AGO - Indigenous spoon made of coconut shell

AGBOIN - The traditional name for Emago community

ATABAKOKO - Large fish pond owned by the Ebutu Family in Idema

ASAGA - The traditional name for Agada community

AYE - The traditional name for Idema community

EMA	-	Community/Town/Village
ENAI-EMA	-	Spirit of the Community
EBHUGH	-	Clan/Kingdom
EGHUN	-	Family
OGHOL	-	Compound/Lineage
OKUKWA	-	A small farmland by the river bank that is close to the Community held permanently by a family member for farming
OLILA	-	Chief or rich man
OLILA-OTU	-	Compound or House Chief, the traditional head of a House
OLILA-EMA	-	The traditional head of a community
OLILA-EBHUGH	-	The Traditional head of a kingdom or clan (King)
OBETIRE	-	The central village square
KUGBO	-	A sub-Clan within Abureni comprising Emago, Amoroto, Akani, Ebililagh etc. presently located in Abua/Odual LGA, Rivers State
IDUMA	-	A sub-clan within Abureni comprising Iduma, Idema, Eboh, Obeduma, Emalo, Oboghe, Oruan, Abu, etc. presently located in Ogbia LGA, Bayelsa State
IGULA	-	Community meeting House
EGHANA	-	Land in the dept of the forest less often cultivated
IKPU	-	Land in the dept of the forest often cultivated.

ESUWA	-	Hoe
OGIDI	-	Matchet
EGHELEGHEL	-	A basket like fishing trap made of raffia
OKEMEGHA-AMUNU-		Hard oil
OKPOROGUM	-	unwidened canoe made for pounding of cooked palm fruits for palm oil production
OBOLO	-	Mud fish. A type of fish specie found in the fresh water Area
ONUNU	-	Srew pine
OBAGHAGHA	-	Crocodile
SAKA	-	Another name for the Odual people
NEW CALABAR	-	The name given by the colonial masters and early administrators to Kalabari
OBHIETIA	-	The traditional name for Obiata
OGBOMASAGA	-	The traditional name for Sangapiri
OKPOKIDUMA	-	Lit. means Iduma money. The Manilla served at some time as a medium of exchange.
OKPOIN	-	Large tripod pot made of iron used for industrial Cooking
IGBA-AMIN	-	A casket of gin consisting of twelve (12) bottles
OKOBA	-	Cowrie
EYAL	-	Festival

OGHAN - The traditional name for Akani community

OBO-AGBOIN - The traditional name for Kugbo

IKEI - Elders

SELECTED BIBILIOGRAPHY

A. PUBLISHED SOURCES:

Achebe, Chinua, *The Trouble with Nigeria*, Enugu, Fourth Dimension Publishing Co. Ltd., (1983)

Achebe, Chinua, *There was a country: A personal history of Biafra*, Great Britain, Allen Lane, (2012)

Achike, Okay, *Ground work of Military Law and Military Rule in Nigeria*, Enugu, Fourth Dimension Publishing Co. Ltd., (1980)

Afigbo, A. E., *The warrant Chiefs: Indirect Rule in South Eastern Nigeria 1891- 1929*, London, Longman Group Ltd., (1972)

Agbu, Osita, Oil and the National Question in Nigeria: The External Dimensions in *Nigerian Journal of International Affairs*, Vol. 26, No.1, (2000)

Alagoa, E. J., *The Small Brave City State: A History of Nembe – Bras s in the Niger Delta*, Ibadan, I. U. P., (1964)

Alagoa, E. J. *A History of the Niger Delta: An Historical Interpretati on of Oral Tradition*, Ibadan, I. U. P., (1972)

Alagoa, E. J. "Ke: The history of an old Delta Community" in *Od uma*, Vol. 2 No. 1. Port Harcourt, Rivers State Council for Arts and Culture, (1974)

Alagoa, E. J. "The Niger Delta States and their Neighbours" in *History of West Africa*, eds, J.F.A. Ajayi and Crowde r Vol. 1, U.K., Longman Group Ltd, (1976)

Alagoa, E. J., *The Ijaw in the New Millennium*, Port Harcourt, Ony oma Research Publications, (1999)

Alagoa, E. J., *The practice of History in Africa: A history of African Historiography*, Port Harcourt, Onyoma Research publica tions, (2006)

Alagoa, E. J., *The Izon of the Niger Delta*, Port Harcourt, Onyoma Research Publications, (2009)

Alkali, M. N., et al, eds. *Nigeria in the Transition years 1993 – 199 9*, Abuja, Presidential Advisory Committee, (1999)

Amadi, Elechi and Opubo, Daminabo, "The Nigerian Civil War " in *Land and peoples of Nigeria: Rivers State*, eds, E. J. Ala goa and Tekenah N. Tamuno, Port Harcourt, Riverside Communications Ltd., (1989)

Anderson, M. G. "Visual Arts" in *Land and People of Bayelsa State : Central Niger Delta*, eds. E. J. Alagoa, Port Harcourt, Onyoma Research Publications, (1999)

Asiegbu, J. U. J., *Nigeria and its British Invaders, 1851 – 1920*, Enugu, Nok Publishers Intl., (1984)

Elaigwu, J. I., *Military Rule and Federalism in Foundations of the Nigerian Federation 1960 – 1995*, eds. J. I. Elaigwu and R. A. Akindele, Jos, IGSR, (2001)

Etekpe, Ambily et al, *Harold Dappa Biriye: His contributions to Politics in Nigeria*, ed. E. J. Alagoa, Port Harcourt, Onyoma Research Publications, (2004)

Fiofori, Tam et al, eds. *Ijo Footprints: Ijo Contributions to Nigeria and the World*, Port Harcourt Onyoma Research Publications (2009)

Ilagha, Nengi Josef, ed., *Landmark Speeches, DSP Alamieyeseigha*, vol. 2 Yenagoa, Treasure Communications Resources Ltd., (2002)

Iloeje, N. P., *A New Geography of Nigeria* (1965)

Jega, A. M., "The Political Economy of Nigeria Federalism" in *Foundation of Nigerian Federalism 1960 – 1995*, eds, J. I. Elaigwu and R. A. Akindele, Jos, IGSR, (2001)

Jones, D. H., "Problems of African Chronology"in *Journal of African History* Vol. XL, No. 2. (1970)

Madiebo, A. Alexander, *The Nigerian Revolution and the Biafran War*, Enugu, Fourth Dimension Publishing Co. Ltd, (1980)

Mbitu, J. S., *African Religions and Philosophy*. London, Heinnemann Education Books Ltd., (1969)

Naanen Ben, and A. I. Pepple "State Movements" in *Land and People of Nigeria: Rivers State*, eds. E. J. Alagoa and T. N. Tamuno, Port Harcourt, Riverside Communications, (1989)

Nnoli, Okwudibia, "Ethnic and Regional Balancing" in *Foundations of Nigerian Federalism 1960 – 1995*, eds, J. I. Elaigwu and R. A. Akindele, Jos, IGSR, (2001)

Nwankwo, Arthur, *Nigeria: The challenge of Biafra*, Enugu, Fourth Dimension Publishers, (1972)

Obasanjo, Olusegun, *My Command*, Ibadan, Heinneman, (1980)

Okonjo, I. M., *British Administration in Nigeria 1900 – 1950*, New York, Nok Publishers, (1974)

Okoko, Kimse and A. Lazarus, "The creation of Bayelsa State" in *Land and People of Bayelsa State: Central Niger Delta*, ed, E. J. Alagoa, Port Harcourt, Onyoma Research Publications, (1999)

Ogan, Charles, *Alfred Diete-Spiff: A Legacy of Development in the Niger Delta*, Port Harcourt, Onyoma Research Publications, (2012)

Rivers State Local Government Law, (1980) (No. 4 of 1981)

Rivers State of Nigeria Official Gazette Vol. 15, No. 16, 25 August (1983)

Rodney, Walter, *How Europe Underdeveloped Africa*, Washington D. C. Howard University Press (1974)

Rooney, D. I. and E. Halladay, *The Building of Modern Africa*, London, George G. Harrap Co. Ltd, (1967)

Sklar, R. L., *Nigerian Political Parties*, Enugu, Nok Publishers, (1983)

Tamuno, T. N., *Oil Wars in the Niger Delta 1849 – 2009*, Ibadan, Stirling Horden Publishers Ltd., (2011)

Ukelonu, O., *Report of the Commission of Inquiry into the Nembe Chieftaincy Dispute*, Enugu, ERN official document no. 24 (1960)

Wariboko, W. E., Social and Political Development in *Land and People of Nigeria: Rivers State, eds.* E. J. Alagoa and T. N. Tamuno, Port Harcourt, Riverside Communications (1989)

Wariboko, W. E., The Emasculation and Transformation of Indigenous governance and structure on the Eastern Niger Delta 1848 – 1960 in *History Concourse 2007; The Future of the Niger Delta: the search for relevant narratives, eds.* Abi Alabo Derefaka and Atei M. Okorobia, Port Harcourt, Onyoma Research Publications, (2009)

Willink, Henry, et al *Report of the Commission Appointed to Inquire into the Fears of the Minorities and the Means of Allaying Them*, London, Her Majesty's Stationery Office, (1958)

B. UNPUBLISHED INTELLIGENCE REPORTS

Dickinson, E. N., *Intelligence Report of the Administrative Structure of Nembe Clan*, 1932

C. OTHER UNPUBLISHED SOURCES

Daniel, C. E., *An Economic and Political History of Idema, From Early Times to Present*, B.A., History Thesis, University of Port Harcourt, (1985)

Egiri, C. E., *Palm Oil Production and Marketing in the Ogbia and Nembe Areas of Rivers State*, B. A. History Thesis, University of Port Harcourt, (1983)

Khadijat, Afolabi, *Impact of Oil Export on Economic Growth in Nigeria from 1970 – 2006*, research work (2011)

Obanobhan Ogbia Constitution (2011) as amended

Ogbia Brotherhood Constitution (2008) as amended

Webber, A. F. C., (Pursuant Judge) Judgement of the Supreme Court of the Protectorate of Southern Nigeria (Calabar Division) in the case of *Chief Dick Harry Braide and Ors v Chief Egbelu and Alagoa* delivered on Monday 3rd March, 1913 obtained from The National Archives Enugu.

Index

1

1979 Constitution · 171, 176

A

Abacha · 174, 175, 176, 177, 178, 222, 223, 226, 228
abafu · 94
abarah · 89
Abayelsa · 221
Abba · 287
Abbe · 196
Abigo · 70, 291
Abiola · 175, 176
Aboko · v, 188
Abonnema · 17, 98, 114, 140, 142, 145, 268
Abu · 44, 53, 189, 295
Abua · 21, 41, 48, 49, 215, 245, 295
Abuloma · 41, 42, 291
abura · 70
Abureni · x, xi, xiv, 16, 20, 21, 22, 24, 30, 42, 48, 49, 53, 83, 93, 97, 126, 130, 131, 136, 186, 189, 190, 191, 193, 197, 207, 228, 233, 234, 249, 252, 253, 254, 255, 256, 257, 258, 259, 260, 261, 264, 265, 278, 282, 294, 295
Abureni Evangelical Outreach · 260
Achebe, Chinua · 166, 217, 248, 297
Achike · 160, 161, 297

Action Group · 134, 135, 136, 155, 160
Ada · 291
Adaafa · 285
Adewari · vi, 86, 179, 180, 284, 292, 293
Adiboko · 20, 38, 81, 189, 190, 231
adrum · 94
Afigbo · 297
Africa Centric · 170
African hoe · 61
Agada · 60, 115, 207, 294
Agadi · 38
Agbu · 205, 206, 297
Agiakoro · 43
Agrisaba · 20, 22, 26, 27, 28, 191, 197, 245
Aguiyi-Ironsi · 164, 165, 166, 181, 211
akain · 25, 67
Akani · 21, 44, 191, 244, 245, 258, 295, 296
Akara masquerade · 257
Akari · 145
Akariosu · 38
Akassa War · xiii, 109, 110, 112, 113, 116, 117
Ake · v, 39, 43, 46, 145, 288
AKE · 285
Akindele · 152, 182, 298, 299
Akintola, Samuel L · 160, 162, 164
Akipelai · 246, 256
AKPANA · 285
Akuku Toru · 267

262

Alagoa · iv, xi, 27, 28, 30, 32, 36, 48, 86, 97, 124, 126, 156, 157, 164, 222, 238, 239, 255, 262, 280, 297, 298, 299, 300, 301
Alamieyeseigha · 224, 225, 229, 298
alata · 70
Alkali · 222, 298
Allagoa, Chief · 26, 127, 129, 130, 264, 270
Aloki · 51, 56, 188, 283, 284
Amadi · 164, 298
Amaegbe · vi, 291
Amorokeni · 21, 38, 244, 245
Amoroto · 244, 245, 295
amulets · 113
Anderson · 86, 298
Ankrah · 166
Apollo, Ekine · 66, 290
Arab oil embargo · 202
Arugu · 47, 145
Asiegbu · 98, 99, 111, 298
Atabakoko · 74
Atigha · 285
Atubo · 18, 21, 60, 115, 207, 215
Awo · 33, 35, 42, 43, 44, 45, 46, 53, 54, 55, 233, 281
Awolowo · 134, 160
axe · 61, 70, 294
Aye · 281, 283, 294
Ayeni · 225
Ayun · 39, 44, 46, 53, 274
Ayun-Amorokoin · 44, 53, 274
Azikiwe · 134, 159, 163

B

banana · 60, 61, 62, 76
Bassambiri · 30, 56, 102, 115, 116, 191, 197, 244, 245, 246, 248, 263, 266, 267, 291, 292
Bayelsa State · xiii, 16, 17, 21, 22, 86, 177, 221, 222, 223, 224, 226, 227, 228, 229, 230, 233, 235, 236, 245, 246, 247, 253, 255, 260, 274, 277, 292, 295, 298, 299
Balewa, Abubakar Tafawa · 159, 161, 163, 164
Biafra · 157, 166, 167, 168, 169, 182, 183, 212, 213, 297, 299
Biafran Forces · 201
Biafran War · 152, 299
Biriye, Harold Dappa · 157, 298
Bonny · 124
Braide · 26, 127, 129, 130, 264, 270
Brass · 15, 18, 26, 27, 93, 95, 97, 98, 100, 101, 105, 109, 111, 114, 124, 125, 127, 129, 133, 136, 137, 140, 141, 184, 186, 190, 191, 193, 194, 195, 196, 207, 216, 222, 227, 266, 267, 268, 270, 297
Brass Division · 125, 184, 186
Buhari, Muhammadu · 173, 192, 193
building · 19, 47, 69, 91, 123, 146, 155, 242, 300

C

Calabar · 26, 124, 128, 129, 270, 301

263

canoe carving · 115, 237
cassava · 60
Chief Dick Harry Braide · 270, 301
Chief Egbelu · 270, 301
Chieftaincy Dispute · 26, 126, 300
claries lazera · 75
cocoyam · 60, 61, 62, 65, 76
cocoyams · 97
colonial authorities · 109, 126, 137, 147, 275
Commission of Inquiry · 26, 126, 267, 300
cooking · 19, 66, 102, 271
cophira · 70
cowrie shell · 76

D

Daminabo, Opubo · 164, 298
Daniel · 2, iii, xi, 63, 69, 72, 75, 99, 113, 133, 143, 145, 233, 290, 291, 292, 301
Dasuki Report · 193, 194, 195
Degema · 124, 190, 191, 270
Derefaka, Abi Alabo · 139, 144, 300
Derri · 244, 245
Diete-Spiff, Alfred Papareye · 166, 167, 181, 182, 186, 300
Dimka · 171
Diya, Oladipo · 175

E

Eastern Region · 26, 126, 133, 134, 135, 136, 165, 168, 181, 182, 200, 211
Ebala Kingdom · 274
Ebilailagh · 21
Ebo · 38, 40, 82, 115, 180, 183, 184, 188, 231
Eboh · 18, 21, 35, 37, 38, 39, 40, 43, 45, 46, 53, 54, 55, 63, 133, 164, 183, 186, 191, 198, 201, 212, 234, 242, 258, 281, 285, 290, 293, 295
Ebutu · 74, 188, 284, 294
Edoghotu · 134, 269, 293
Edumanom · 22, 254
Edumollogbo, Lionel · 291
Efere, E.E. · 30, 255
Egbelu · 26, 127, 129, 130, 264, 270
Egberike · 224, 225
egheleghel · 69, 75
Eghun-Otu · 22, 77
Eghunuma · 38, 41, 42, 43, 45, 46, 54, 281, 289
Egiri · 29, 184, 187, 188, 301
Ejituwu, Nkparom · 139
Ekelekpum · 257
Ekere · 44, 47, 288, 292
Ekineba, 86
Ekine Society · 49, 85, 86, 87, 88
Ekule · 27
Elaigwu, J.I., · 152, 153, 176, 182, 298, 299
Emago-Kugbo · 244, 245, 255, 258, 259, 292

Emagu · 145
Emalo · 18, 21, 186, 198, 215, 295
Ematadu · 186
Ene · 283
Enemugwem · 139
English Language · 207
environmental degradation · 224, 250, 277
Etekpe · 157, 298
eyal odudul · 83, 147, 256
eyal-ilobhiri · 83

F

farming · 19, 58, 59, 61, 62, 63, 68, 80, 89, 115, 139, 141, 199, 203, 205, 237, 255, 256, 294
Federal Capital Territory · 170
Federation of Nigeria · 151
Fenibo · 36, 37, 38, 41, 45, 51, 54, 56, 281
Fiofori, Tam · 298
fishing · 68, 69, 71, 73, 74, 139, 143, 199, 203, 204, 205, 216, 237, 255, 295
fresh water crab · 75

G

Gamble · 101, 103
Godspower · 286
Godswill · 272, 293
Goldie · 108, 123, 124

Gowon · 165, 168, 169, 181, 185, 211
Great Britain · 158

H

Happy · 214
Hill · 99, 100
Horton, Robin · iv
Hunting · xii, 71

I

Ibanichuka, Ado VI, 123
Ibe · 145, 246, 258
Ibem · 38, 40
Ibhughom · 145
Idah · 287
Idema · v, 18, 20, 21, 22, 23, 24, 25, 26, 27, 28, 29, 30, 35, 36, 38, 40, 41, 42, 45, 63, 66, 67, 68, 69, 71, 72, 75, 76, 81, 82, 86, 99, 113, 115, 127, 131, 133, 140, 143, 145, 146, 179, 180, 183, 184, 186, 187, 188, 189, 190, 191, 195, 198, 201, 206, 207, 208, 212, 217, 218, 228, 230, 231, 242, 243, 244, 245, 246, 247, 248, 249, 258, 259, 263, 269, 270, 272, 281, 289, 290, 291, 292, 293, 294, 295, 301
Idema · 24, 128, 281, 283
Iduma · v, vi, x, xi, xiii, xiv, 15, 16, 17, 18, 19, 20, 21, 22, 25, 26, 27, 28, 29, 30, 32, 33, 35, 37, 38, 39, 40, 41

265

, 42, 43, 45, 47, 48, 49, 50, 51, 52, 53, 54, 55, 56, 57, 58, 62, 63, 67, 6 9, 71, 74, 75, 76, 77, 81, 82, 87, 91 , 92, 93, 95, 96, 98, 109, 113, 114, 115, 116, 117, 118, 119, 122, 125, 127, 133, 136, 137, 138, 139, 140, 141, 144, 145, 147, 148, 150, 152, 178, 179, 180, 181, 182, 183, 186, 187, 188, 189, 190, 191, 192, 193, 195, 196, 197, 198, 199, 200, 201, 203, 205, 206, 207, 208, 209, 210, 212, 213, 214, 215, 217, 218, 219, 223, 226, 227, 228, 229, 233, 234, 235, 236, 237, 240, 241, 242, 243, 244, 245, 248, 249, 250, 251, 252, 253, 254, 256, 257, 258, 259, 261, 262, 263, 264, 265, 266, 267, 268, 269, 270, 271, 272, 273, 274, 275, 276, 277, 278, 279, 281, 282, 289, 294, 295, 296

Iduma · 1, 92, 122, 151, 221, 281, 29 5

Idumanamugbo · 36, 37, 45, 54, 281

Igbo country · 120

Igbo Union · 155

Igbos · 165, 181, 217

Igoniwari · v, 36, 38, 39, 40, 41, 45, 4 6, 51, 56, 82, 179, 230, 231, 263, 2 83, 284, 289

Ikata · 287

Ikei-Otu · 150

Ikio · 50, 149

Ikokosi · 63, 290

ikoloman · 68

Ikoni · 38, 56, 283, 284

ikpisikpisi · 67

Ikpoku · 38, 56, 188, 283, 284

Ikpu · 59, 60, 61

Ikuli · 284

Ikuli-Ene · 140, 292

Ilagha · 225, 298

Iloeje · 18, 299

Inko · 188

Ipian · 288

ipoki · 74

ire · 70

iroko osa · 70

iseleguma · 67

Isoko · 199

itita · 65, 68, 73

Ivi · 38, 234, 293

J

Jackson · 255, 292

Jaja · 106

Jega, Attahiru · 152, 299

Joel · 66, 71, 81, 213, 231, 235, 281, 290

Johnson · 67, 68, 75, 106, 145, 164, 1 81, 211, 226, 290, 291

Jonathan · 234, 246

Jones · 32, 299

K

Kalabari · 15, 16, 47, 48, 49, 50, 51, 5 3, 62, 69, 72, 76, 86, 91, 122, 127,

258, 261, 268, 269, 271, 274, 275, 278, 296
Ke · v, 28, 33, 35, 36, 45, 47, 48, 51, 5 5, 268, 274, 281, 289, 297
Khadijat · 202, 301
Kingibe · 175
Kirk · 110, 112
Koko, Frederick William, Mingi VIII · 1 09, 110, 112
Kolo · 40, 294
Koru · v, 38, 145, 198, 252, 289
Kugbo · 17, 21, 22, 26, 30, 38, 75, 76, 127, 183, 212, 213, 214, 254, 255, 259, 267, 270, 278, 296

L

logging · 199, 237

M

Macdonald · 99, 108
Madiebo · 157, 159, 161, 299
maize · 60, 62
masquerade displays · 49
matchet · 61, 84, 232
Mbitu · 257, 299
melon · 60
military coup d'etat · 192
mitragyna ciliate ibhogh · 70
mud fish · 74, 75

N

Naanem · 156, 299
National Census · 197
National Council of Nigeria and the C ameroons · 155
National Republican Convention · 17 4
National Youth Service Corps · 169
Native Authority · 125, 126
Native Court · 126, 131, 132
nauches diderrichis opepe · 70
Nembe · 16, 17, 20, 22, 26, 27, 29, 33 , 39, 44, 45, 49, 51, 55, 56, 62, 69, 72, 76, 91, 95, 96, 97, 98, 101, 104 , 109, 110, 111, 113, 114, 115, 116 , 117, 122, 123, 126, 127, 128, 130 , 131, 132, 140, 141, 182, 184, 186 , 191, 193, 196, 197, 207, 227, 243 , 244, 245, 246, 247, 248, 251, 252 , 258, 261, 262, 263, 264, 265, 266 , 267, 268, 270, 275, 276, 278, 292 , 294, 297, 300, 301
New Calabar · 15, 16, 122
Niger · xi, 18, 25, 27, 28, 30, 31, 32, 3 6, 48, 86, 92, 93, 97, 99, 101, 104, 105, 106, 108, 109, 110, 111, 112, 114, 117, 118, 123, 124, 125, 135, 138, 139, 144, 148, 157, 166, 208, 222, 224, 236, 238, 249, 255, 275, 280, 297, 298, 299, 300
Niger Delta · xi, 18, 25, 27, 28, 30, 31, 32, 36, 48, 86, 112, 135, 139, 144, 148, 157, 166, 208, 222, 224, 236,

267

238, 239, 249, 255, 280, 297, 298, 299, 300
Niger Protectorate · 105
Nigeria Civil War · 152, 211, 276
Nigeria National Alliance · 162
Nigerian Agip Oil Company · 210
Nigerian Army · 161, 201, 215, 216
Nnoli · 182, 299
Northern Ijaw · 185
Northern Peoples Congress · 134, 155, 160
Nwankwo · 167, 168, 299
Nzeogwu · 164, 181

O

Oath of Allegiance · 80
Obanobhan Ogbia Constitution · 253, 301
Obasanjo · 168, 171, 211, 299
OBE · 287
Obeduma · v, 18, 21, 33, 35, 38, 42, 43, 44, 45, 47, 53, 54, 55, 115, 133, 136, 186, 191, 197, 198, 207, 213, 214, 230, 232, 233, 242, 249, 250, 289, 290, 292, 293, 295
Obeten · 43, 44
Obhietia · 60, 115
obhom · 70
Obiata · 60, 115, 207, 296
Obodiri · 38, 41, 56, 188, 231, 283, 284, 290
Obodom · 38, 40, 41

Oboghe · 18, 21, 113, 186, 198, 215, 292, 295
Obomuotu · 41
Ode · 232
Odiase · 242
Odioma · 17, 28, 261, 272, 278
Odo · 287
Odu · 76, 188, 291
Odual · 15, 17, 21, 26, 39, 46, 48, 49, 52, 53, 75, 76, 126, 127, 130, 215, 245, 261, 265, 267, 271, 272, 274, 278, 295, 296
Offor · iii, 63, 68, 69, 133, 213, 232, 234, 272, 290
Ogan, Charles · 168, 181, 182, 186, 300
Ogbia · xiv, 15, 16, 17, 21, 29, 30, 42, 48, 49, 51, 53, 93, 97, 126, 130, 136, 184, 191, 192, 193, 195, 196, 197, 198, 199, 201, 222, 226, 227, 229, 241, 242, 245, 251, 252, 253, 254, 265, 266, 274, 277, 278, 295, 301
Ogbomade · 133, 226, 227
Oghilolo · 200, 201
Oghol-Otu · xiii, 22, 80
Ogidi · 227, 258, 292
Ogidi-Ene · 227
ogie · 94
Ogio · 27
ogionan · 86
Ogiri · 287
Ogolom · 149
Ogonokom · 41
Ogu · 38, 56, 188, 283, 284

oil boom · 152, 200, 202, 203, 205
Oil Rivers Protectorate · 123
Ojukwu · 165, 167, 168, 181, 182, 212
Okara · 228
Okeinodo · 41
Okeke · 287
okemegha · 64, 94, 95
okemegha amunu · 64
Okiki · 39, 40, 46, 52
Okikiayun · 53, 115
Okilo, Melford · 136, 137, 190, 192, 207, 252, 292
Okiori · 234, 286
Okoko, · 222, 299
Okoma · 36, 54
Okoni · 76, 145, 291
Okonjo · 299
Okoroba · 17, 20, 26, 27, 28, 183, 191, 197, 215, 244, 245, 254, 256, 258, 259, 278
Okorobia · 30, 139, 144, 300
Okorobo · 21, 22, 254
okpoin · 94
Okpoma · 28, 194
okporogum · 64, 94
Okrika · 42, 62, 69, 76, 101, 123
Okrika-Ijaws · 42
okukwa · 60
okunu (system) · 63, 94, 95
Olilaema · v, 36, 38, 39, 40, 41, 42, 44, 45, 47, 80, 82, 83, 84, 150, 179, 188, 228, 230, 231, 233, 234, 289
Ologo · 38, 234, 285
Oluasiri · 186, 193, 195, 244, 245

Omongi · 35, 36, 37, 45, 49, 51, 54, 56, 281
Onbu · 287
Onitsha bloc · 217
onunu · 68
Operation Feed the Nation · 204
Opume · 246, 256
Opuso · v, 35, 38, 43, 44, 45, 46, 51, 53, 54, 55, 115, 116, 232, 233, 287, 289
Orlu, Samuel· 47, 288, 290
Oral tradition · 31, 93, 120, 140
Oruama · 41, 42, 43, 46
Oruan · 18, 21, 60, 113, 115, 145, 215, 292, 295
Osoko · 39, 52
Osomu · 283
Otolo · 284
Otuabagi · 17, 261, 273, 278
Otuogba · 29, 200, 201
Owerri bloc · 217
Owerri Province · 125, 157
Oyakhilome, Fidelis · 192
Ozibh-Onyeke · 200
Ozil · 285

P

palm oil and kernel · 15, 63, 93, 199, 200, 201, 202, 203, 205, 237, 275
pepper · 40, 41, 60
pit props · 19
plantain · 60, 61, 62, 65, 76, 97, 180
political class · 121, 278

pomade · 66
Port Harcourt · 2, iv, v, x, 27, 29, 30, 42, 75, 124, 137, 139, 144, 157, 164, 166, 182, 185, 186, 189, 196, 201, 209, 217, 218, 255, 259, 280, 291, 292, 297, 298, 299, 300, 301
pre-colonial era · xii, xiii, 58, 77, 204
Provisional Ruling Council · 223

Q

Queen Elizabeth II · 158

R

raffia products · 205, 237
red mangrove tree · 19
Regent · 180, 183, 184, 288
Rivers Chiefs and People Conference · 157
Rivers State · 2, 21, 22, 27, 29, 30, 42, 70, 124, 135, 136, 156, 164, 167, 181, 182, 184, 185, 189, 190, 191, 193, 195, 196, 198, 204, 207, 208, 218, 226, 228, 245, 252, 267, 291, 295, 297, 298, 299, 300, 301
Rodney · 118, 119, 300
Rooney · 123, 300
Royal Niger Company · 92, 97, 99, 105, 106, 109, 112, 114, 117, 118, 123, 124, 125, 275
Rufus · 285

S

Sacrifice Island · 101
salt making · 19
Santa Barbara Oilfield, 242
Senior Special Assistant · 234
SETRACO · 247
Shagari, Shehu Aliyu · 172
Shell Petroleum Development Company · 210, 241, 242, 245, 248, 249
Shonekan, Ernest · 174
Sklar · 134, 300
snake-fish · 75
Social Democratic Party · 174
Soku · 17, 241, 268, 269
Southern Ijaw · 185, 222
sugarcane · 60

T

Talbot · 25
Tamuno, Tekena Nitonye · 30, 112, 124, 156, 164, 298, 299, 300
The National Archives Enugu · 301
The Times · 105
Trans Atlantic palm oil trade · 119
tripod pot · 94, 296
Twon · 28, 104, 126, 186

U

Ukelonu · 126, 300
United Middle Belt Congress · 158
United Progressive Grand Alliance · 162
Urhobo · 199, 201
USA · 202

V

vegetable · 143

W

Wariboko · 124, 144, 148, 300

water yam · 60
Webber · 25, 128, 270, 271, 301
West Africa · 28, 297
Western House of Assembly · 160
Wills · 263, 292
Williamson, Kay · 30, 48, 255, 280
wrestling contests · 50, 256

X

xenomystus · 74, 75

Y

Yamaha · 209

www.ingramcontent.com/pod-product-compliance
Lightning Source LLC
Chambersburg PA
CBHW052133010526
44113CB00035B/2041